Dictionary of
1000 French Proverbs

With English Equivalents

D1615648

Dictionary of
1000 French Proverbs
With English Equivalents

Peter Mertvago

HIPPOCRENE BOOKS
New York

For information, address:
HIPPOCRENE BOOKS, INC.
171 Madison Avenue
New York, NY 10016

Cataloging-in-Publication Data

Mertvago. Peter.
    Dictionary of 1000 French proverbs : with English equivalents /
Peter Mertvago.
        p.   cm.
    Includes bibliographical references.
    ISBN 0-7818-0400-0
    1. Proverbs. French. 2. Proverbs. French—Translations into
English. I. Title.
PN6451.M47   1996   95-51083
398.9'41—dc20   CIP

Printed in the United States of America.

To Pica

Acknowledgment

The author wishes to thank
Brigitte Andrèassier-Pearl
for her invaluable assistance in preparing and
proofreading the manuscript for publication.

Introduction

Proverbs and Language

It has been said that nothing more aptly summarizes the characteristics of a people or nation than proverbs, which epitomize its wisdom, temperament and outlook on life. Efforts to justify such a premise of the prominence of national characterization of proverbs involve a quasi "Darwinian" approach to the transmission of proverbs that would have one believe that only those which appeal to a people *en masse* survive.

However theoretically attractive this view may be, a comparison of the proverbs of different nations shows that it is not valid. Human nature and the human condition are essential constants not prone to alteration by geopolitical or even linguistic differences.[1] Proverbs address the day-to-day realities of this condition, the world as it is and as it is perceived through human eyes. They may be contradictory insofar as those realities themselves are contradictory. But the speaker of a proverb does no more than make an empirical statement about things as they are. It may be up to the poet to address things as they could, should or might be. In the Bible, this is the difference between

---

1   This is the conclusion drawn by Champion after thoroughly studying the proverbial folklore of 193 peoples, when he observed that "all the civilization of the ages could not eradicate the primary instincts of mankind," and that proverbial wisdom was the same the world over, differing only in the rendering." Champion, S.G. *Racial Proverbs*, (New York:1963), p. xxiv.

Solomon's *Book of Proverbs* and his *Song of Songs*. An accurate portrait of a people, if indeed any at all is possible, may perhaps be sought in a superimposition of the two views, the prosaic and the poetic, the pedestrian and the artistic.[2]

From a linguistic point of view, if languages are considered to be semiotic systems which communicate information by means of *signs* or *semeia* that stand for specific ideas, objects or situations in the real world, proverbs function as complex units which dispense a speaker from the need of any prior formulation of concepts that are already current in a ready-made form in his or her cultural group. This is borne out by the Latin etymology of the word given by the OED: *pro* + *verbum* (word) + *ium* (collective suffix) hence meaning "a (recognized) set of words put forth."

The French Proverb

To the extent that there is a uniform pool of human experience and interborrowing from common historical and cultural antecedents, the French proverb is largely a French counterpart of similar expressions that are intrinsic to European and even universal folk-lore. This commonality of expression within Europe goes back to the interborrowing which resulted from the rampant translation of proverbs after the publication in 1500 of Erasmus' *Adages*, that produced what had been termed an "international medieval" class of proverbs which derive from Latin and owe their currency to that international language of the Middle Ages.[3]

---

2   Roy, C., "La sagesse des nations" in *L'homme en question* (Paris: 1960), p. 44.

3   *Gemeinmittelalterlich* is the term used by F. Seiler to describe this large category of proverbs, in *Deutsche Sprichwöterkunde*, Handbuch des deutschen Unterrichts IV.III (Munich: 1922), cited in Taylor, *The Proverb* (Cambridge: 1931), pp. 50-51.

Consequently, for a student of French or anyone else wishing to communicate effectively in the language, the most common proverbs should be understood and learnt in the same way that idioms and individual words are to be mastered. This is facilitated by a clear appreciation of the degree of overlap with and differences from the common pool of proverbs which has been described above.

How to Use This Book

This book is a selective collection of what in the opinion of the author make up the 1000 most important and commonly used and understood proverbs of written and spoken French. It is neither an exhaustive compilation nor does it include proverbs that may be current in specific overseas French-speaking regions or countries, as in Canada or Africa, to the exclusion of the metropolitan France. That in itself would be an interesting subject for comparative study but transcends the scope of this book.

The entries have been arranged as in a dictionary, in alphabetical order by French key word and numbered consecutively from 1 to 1000. For the purposes of this book, a *key word* is the sequentially first noun most closely associated with the meaning of the proverb and/or having a greater linguistic range or frequency. For proverbs without nouns, key words may be verbs, adjectives or adverbs used on the basis of the same considerations. Alternate variations of proverbs or alternate words or phrases used in the same proverb are placed within parentheses in the entry that represents the most common form of the proverb.

An important distinction is made in providing the English equivalents of the proverbs. For many French proverbs there is an exact or nearly exact word-for-word equivalent in English where the same proverb exists in both languages in an identical or easily recognizable and closely-related alternate form. In such cases, the English proverb appears below the French entry in normal type.

But where no lexically-equivalent proverb exists in English, rather than provide a translation of the French, the book offers actual English proverbs[4] that would be used in similar contexts or circumstances. This is consistent with the treatment of proverbs as semiotic units that communicate entire thoughts in an encapsulated, ready-made format. Such equivalents are set in *italics* and it is assumed that the reader, once aware of the meaning or sense of a proverb and if so inclined, may proceed to identify the lexical differences by using standard monolingual or bilingual dictionaries if necessary. English proverbs that have a meaning opposite to that of the French entry may be listed for comparison, in which case they are marked by a dagger [†]. An English Key Word Index is provided to facilitate the use of the book from English into French.

4   For the purposes of this book, English proverbs means either British or American proverbs. British spelling has been used throughout, with the exception of those proverbs whose provenance is recognized as being exclusively American.

A

Abondance	1	Abondance de biens ne nuit pas.
		Store is no sore.

Absent	2	Les absents ont toujours tort.
		The absent are always in the wrong.

Accommodement 3 Un mauvais accommodement vaut mieux qu'un bon procès.
A bad peace is better than a good quarrel.

Acheter 4 Mieux vaut acheter qu'emprunter.
Better buy than borrow.

Acheteur 5 Il y a plus d'acheteurs que de connaisseurs.
There's a sucker born every minute.

6 Il y a plus de fous acheteurs que de fous vendeurs.
There are more foolish buyers than foolish sellers.

Action 7 Une bonne action ne reste jamais sans récompense.
A good deed is never lost.

Activité 8 Activité est mère de prosperité.
Diligence is the mother of good fortune.

Admiration

9 L'admiration est la fille de l'ignorance.
Admiration is the daughter of ignorance.

Adversité

10 L'adversité est la pierre de touche de l'amitié.
Adversity is the touchstone of friendship.

11 L'adversité rend sage.
Adversity makes men wise.

Affection

12 L'affection aveugle la raison.
Affection blinds reason.

Age

13 Chaque âge a ses plaisirs.
Every age wants its playthings.

Agneau

14 Mieux vaut tondre l'agneau que le pourceau.
Go to a goat (ass) for wool. Ask pears of an elm tree.

15 Où le loup trouve un agneau, il y en cherche un nouveau.
The dog returns to where he has been fed.

Aide

16 Un peu d'aide fait grand bien.
Every little bit helps.

Aider

17 Aide-toi et Dieu t'aidera.
God helps those who help themselves.

Aigle

18 L'aigle ne chasse point aux mouches.
Eagles don't catch flies.

19 L'aigle n'engendre pas la colombe.
Eagles don't breed doves.

Aiguille

20 L'on ne peut cacher aiguille en sac.
Fire cannot be hidden in flax.

21 Qui prête son aiguille sans gage en perd l'usage.
Lend your horse and you may have back his skin.

Aimer

22 C'est trop aimer quand on en meurt.
They love too much that die for love.

23 Quand on n'a pas ce que l'on aime, il faut aimer
ce que l'on a.
*Since we cannot get what we like, let us like
what we can get.*

24 Qui aime bien, châtie bien.
He who loves well, chastises well.

25 Qui bien aime tard oublie.
He who loves well will never forget.

Air

26 Qui crache en l'air reçoit le crachat sur soi.
Who spits against the wind, spits in his own face.

Aller

27 Au long aller, petit fardeau pèse.
In a long journey, straw weighs.

28 On ne va jamais si loin que lorsqu'on ne sait pas
où l'on va.
*It's a long road that goes nowhere. The right road is
the shortest road.*

Allouette

29 Faute de froment, les alouettes font leur nid dans
le seigle.
*He that may not do as he would, must do as he
may.*

30 L'allouette en main vaut mieux que l'oie qui vole.
A bird in the hand is worth two in the bush.

Ambition

31 C'est l'ambition qui perd les grands hommes.
Ambition loses many a man.

32 L'ambition ne vieillit pas.
Ambition has no rest.

Amender 33 De ce que l'on peut amender, il ne faut pas trop
s'inquiéter.
Worrying doesn't mend nor pay.

34 Mal vit qui ne s'amende.
Only a fool never changes his mind.

Ami 35 Ami de plusieurs, ami de nul.
*Who has many friends, has no friends. A friend
to all's a friend to none.*

36 Ami de table est variable.
Fair-weather friends are not worth having.

37 Au besoin on connaît l'ami.
A friend in need is a friend indeed.

38 Deux amis à une bourse, l'un chante et l'autre
grousse.
*When two friends have a common purse, one
sings and the other weeps.*

39 Il faut éprouver les amis aux petites occasions et
les employer aux grandes.
First prove your friends before you need them.

40 Il vaut mieux perdre un bon mot qu'un ami.
Better lose a jest than a friend.

41 L'ami par intérêt est une hirondelle sur les toits.
*False friends are like autumn leaves, found every-
where.*

42 Les vieux amis et les vieux écus sont les meilleurs.
Old friends and old wine and old gold are best.

43 Mieux vaut avoir un ami à la cour que de l'argent dans la bourse.
A friend in the market is better than money in the purse.

44 Qui cesse d'être ami ne l'a jamais été.
He never was a friend who has ceased to be one.

45 Si ton ami est borgne, regarde-le de profil.
You love your friends despite their faults. A friend should bear his friend's infirmities.

46 Un bon ami vaut mieux que cent parents.
Friends are to be preferred to relatives.

Amitié

47 Il ne faut pas laisser croître l'herbe sur le chemin de l'amitié.
Let not the grass grow on the path of friendship.

48 L'amitié demande du retour.
Friendship is a two-way street.

49 L'amitié rompue n'est jamais bien soudée.
A broken friendship is never mended.

50 Les petits cadeaux entretiennent l'amitié.
Friendship is a plant that one must often water.

51 Recevoir sans donner fait tourner l'amitié.
Friendship cannot stand all on one side.

Amour

52 Amour apprend aux ânes à danser.
Love makes all burdens light. Love makes a wit of a fool.

53 Après l'amour, le repentir.
The end of passion is the beginning of repentance.

54 L'amour et la pauvreté font ensemble mauvais ménage.
Love lasts as long as money endures.

55 L'amour fait passer le temps et le temps fait passer l'amour.
Love makes time pass, time makes love pass.

56 On revient toujours à ses premières amours.
One always returns to his first love.

57 Qui se marie par amour, a bonnes nuits et mauvais jours.
He who marries for love without money has good nights and sorry days.

An

58 L'an passé est toujours le meilleur.
It's always the biggest one that gets away.

59 Les ans ont beaucoup plus vu que les livres n'en ont connu.
Years know more than books.

Ancre

60 Deux ancres sont bons au navire.
Good riding at two anchors for if one breaks the other may hold.

Ane

61 A laver tête d'un âne on perd son savon.
He who scrubs the head of an ass wastes his soap.

62 L'âne de la montagne porte le vin et boit de l'eau.
Even if the ass is laden with gold, he will seek his food among the thorns. The ass is not more learned though he may be loaded with books.

63 L'âne du commun est toujours le plus mal bâté.
The common horse is worst shod.

Apparence

64 Les apparences sont souvent trompeuses.
Appearances are deceiving.

Appetit

65 L'appétit est le meilleur cuisinier.
Hunger is the best cook.

66 L'appétit vient en mangeant.
    Appetite comes with the eating.

Apprendre

67 Ce n'est pas à un vieux singe qu'on apprend à
    faire des grimaces.
    You can't teach an old dog new tricks.

68 On apprend en faillant.
    We learn by our mistakes.

Arbre

69 Arbre trop souvent transplanté rarement fait fruit
    à planter.
    A tree often transplanted neither grows nor thrives.

70 Chaque arbre se connaît à son fruit.
    A tree is known by its fruit.

71 Faire de l'arbre d'un pressoir le manche d'un cer-
    noir.
    Spoil the horn and make a spoon.

72 Il ne faut pas juger de l'arbre par l'écorce.
    Don't judge a book by its cover.

73 L'arbre cache la forêt.
    Not to see the forest for the trees.

74 L'arbre ne tombe pas du premier coup.
    The first blow does not fell the tree.

75 Quand l'arbre est tombé, chacun court aux
    branches.
    *When the tree is fallen, everyone goes to it with
    his hatchet.*

Argent

76 L'argent est rond pour rouler.
    Money is round and rolls away.

77 L'argent est le nerf de la guerre.
    Money is the sinews of war.

78 L'argent ne fait pas le bonheur.
Money can't buy happiness.

79 Marteau d'argent ouvre porte de fer.
A silver key can open an iron lock.

80 Plaie d'argent n'est pas mortelle.
Health without money is half an ague.

81 Qui a de l'argent a des pirouettes.
Money makes a man laugh.

82 Qui n'a point argent en bourse ait miel en
bouche.
If you have no money in your purse, you must
have honey in your mouth.

Art

83 Ce qu'art ne peut, hasard achève.
Luck is better than science.

84 L'art est de cacher l'art.
Art consists in concealing art.

Artisan

85 Chacun est artisan de sa fortune.
Every man is the architect of his own fortune.

Attendre

86 Tout vient à point à qui peut attendre.
Everything comes to him who waits.

Aune

87 Au bout de l'aune faut le drap.
All things come to an end.

88 Il ne faut pas mesurer les autres à son aune.
Don't judge others by yourself.

Avancer

89 Quand on n'avance pas, on recule.
He who never goes forward goes backwards.

Avare   90 A père avare, enfant (fils) prodigue.
                   A miser's son is a spendthrift.

               91 Les avares font nécessité de tout.
                   Poverty wants many things, and avarice all.

Aveugle   92 Au pays (royaume) des aveugles, les borgnes sont
                   rois.
                   In the land of the blind, the one-eyed are kings.

Avis   93 Deux avis valent mieux qu'un.
                   Two heads are better than one.

               94 L'avis de la femme est de peu de prix, mais qui
                   ne le prend pas est un sot.
                   A woman's advice is no great thing, but he who
                   won't take it is a fool.

Avocat   95 Bon avocat, mauvais voisin.
                   A good lawyer, a bad neighbour.

               96 Le vent n'entre jamais dans la maison d'un avo-
                   cat.
                   Lawyers' houses are built on the heads of fools.

B

Bannière	97	Cent ans bannière, cent ans civière.
		Seven fat years, seven lean years.

Bât	98	Chacun sait (nul ne sait mieux que l'âne) où le bât (le) blesse.
		Everyone knows where his shoe pinches.
		None knows where the shoe pinches like the wearer.

Beauté	99	Beauté sans bonté est comme vin éventé.
		A fair woman without virtue is like palled wine.
	100	On ne va pas avec la beauté de sa femme au moulin.
		Beauty doesn't make the pot boil.

Bénéfice	101	Il faut prendre le bénéfice avec les charges.
		A man must take the fat with the lean.
	102	On ne peut avoir en même temps femme et bénéfice.
		Woman brings to man the greatest blessing and the greatest plague.

Berger	103	Un berger a souvent plus de sens qu'un savant.
		Wisdom doesn't always speak in Greek and Latin.

Bergère

104 Mieux vaut aimer bergères que princesses.
*It is better to have what you cannot love than love
what you cannot have.*

Besoin

105 Besoin fait la vieille trotter (et l'endormi
réveiller).
Need makes the old wife trot.

Bête

106 Deux bêtes paissent bien un pré.
Two can live as cheaply as one.

107 Morte la bête, mort le venin.
Dead men never bite.

108 On prend les bêtes (boeufs) par les cornes et les
hommes par les paroles.
An ox is taken by the horns, and a man by the
tongue.

109 Qui bête va à Rome, tel en retourne.
Who goes a beast to Rome, a beast returns.

110 Qui se fait bête (brebis), le loup le mange.
He that makes himself a sheep shall be eaten by
the wolves.

Beurre

111 On ne peut pas avoir le beurre et l'argent du
beurre.
You can't have your cake and eat it too.

112 On ne saurait manier le beurre qu'on ne s'en
graisse les doigts.
He that measureth oil shall anoint his fingers.

Bien

113 Bien mal acquis ne profite point (jamais).
Ill-gotten goods seldom prosper.

114 Grand bien ne vient pas en peu d'heures.
A strong town is not won in an hour.

115　Nul bien sans peine.
No pain, no gain.

No joy without annoy.

116　Qui est loin de son bien, est près de son dommage.
Far from home, near thy harm.

117　Tout est bien qui finit bien.
All's well that ends well.

Bienfait　118　Un bienfait n'est jamais perdu.
A good deed is never lost.

Blé　119　En petit champ croît bon blé.
Big buckets can be filled at small streams. Good things come in small packages.

Boeuf　120　Dieu donne le boeuf, et non pas la corne.
God gives the milk but not the pail.

121　Faute de boeuf, on fait labourer par son âne.
If you don't have a horse, ride a cow. A man must plough with such oxen as he has.

122　Mieux vaut en paix un oeuf qu'en guerre un boeuf.
Better an egg in peace than an ox in war.

123　On a beau mener le boeuf à l'eau s'il n'a soif.
You can lead a horse to water, but you can't make him drink.

124　Vieux boeuf fait sillon droit.
An old ox makes a straight furrow.

Bois　125　Il n'est feu que de bois vert.
Green wood makes a hot fire.

126 Le bois tordu fait le feu droit.
Crooked logs make straight fires.

127 Tout bois n'est pas bon à faire flèche.
Every block does not make a Mercury.

Boîte 128 Dans les petites boîtes, les bons onguents.
The best things come in small packages.

Bon 129 Bon à tout, bon à rien.
Jack of all trades, master of none.

Bonheur 130 Il n'est point de bonheur sans nuage.
No joy without annoy. Pleasure has a sting in its tail.

131 Le bonheur fuit celui qui le cherche.
Happiness is never found by pursuing it.

Bossu 132 Le bossu ne voit pas sa bosse, mais il voit celle de son confrère.
The hunchback sees not his own hump, but his companion's.

Bouche 133 Bouche qui rit ne blesse personne.
There are few who would rather be hated than laughed at.

134 Ce qui est amer à la bouche est doux au coeur.
That which is bitter to endure may be sweet to remember. The bitter must come before the sweet.

135 En bouche close n'entre mouche.
A closed mouth catches no flies.

136 Il arrive beaucoup de choses entre la bouche et le verre.
There's many a slip 'twixt the cup and the lip.

Boulanger	137	Ne sois pas boulanger si la tête est en beurre.
		He that has a head of wax must not walk in the sun.
Bourse	138	La bourse ouvre la bouche.
		A full purse makes a mouth speak.
		Money talks.
Brebis	139	A brebis tondue, Dieu mesure le vent.
		God tempers the wind to the shorn lamb.
	140	Brebis comptées, le loup les mange.
		The wolf eats often of the sheep that have been told.
	141	Brebis qui bêle perd sa goulée.
		The sheep that bleats loses a mouthful.
	142	Folle et simple est la brebis qui au loup se confesse.
		It is a foolish sheep that makes the wolf his confessor.
	143	Il faut tondre les brebis et non pas les écorcher.
		It is the part of a good shepherd to shear the flock, not flay it.
	144	Il ne faut qu'une brebis galeuse pour gâter un troupeau.
		One scabbed sheep will mar a flock.
	145	Qui se fait brebis, le loup le mange.
		He that makes himself a sheep shall be eaten by the wolves.
Bride	146	Entre bride et l'éperon, de toute choses gît la raison.
		Reason lies between the bridle and the spur.

Buisson   147 Il a battu les buissons et un autre a pris les
                          oiseaux.
                          One beats the bush and another catches the bird.

                     148 Il n'est si petit buisson qui ne porte son ombre.
                          The smallest hair throws its shadow.

Buse   149 On ne saurait faire d'une buse un épervier.
                          A buzzard never makes a good hawk.

C

Cage

150 La belle cage ne nourrit pas l'oiseau.
A fine cage won't feed the hungry bird.

151 Mieux vaut être oiseau de bocage que de cage.
It is the beautiful bird which gets caged.

Cause

152 Les petites causes produisent souvent de grands effets.
Little subjects decide big ones.

153 Il n'y a pas d'effet sans cause.
Take away the cause and the effect must cease.

Chambre

154 Vides chambres font dames folles.
Bare walls make giddy housewives.

Champ

155 En petit champ croît bon blé.
Crooked furrows grow straight corn.

Changement

156 Chance passe science.
Luck is better than science.

Chapon

157 Qui chapon mange, chapon lui vient.
Money begets money. They that have, get.

Charbonnier 158 Charbonnier est maître chez soi.
Every man is a master in his own house.

Charité 159 Charité bien ordonnée commence chez soi.
Charity begins at home.

Charrette 160 Vieille charrette crie à chaque tour.
Old vessels must leak.

Charretier 161 Il n'est si bon charretier qui ne verse.
It's a fine horse that never stumbles.

Chasse 162 Qui va à la chasse perd sa place.
If you leave your place, you lose it.

Chasser 163 Qui deux choses chasse, ni l'une ni l'autre ne prend.
He who chases two hares, catches neither.

Chasseur 164 A jeune chasseur, il faut vieux chien.
For a young trooper, and old horse.

Chat 165 A bon chat, bon rat.
To a good cat, a good rat.

166 Chat (chien) échaudé craint l'eau froide.
A scalded cat fears cold water.

167 Jamais chat emmitouflé ne prit souris.
A muffled cat never caught a mouse.

168 Il ne faut pas (r)éveiller le chat qui dort.
Let sleeping dogs lie.

169 Il ne faut pas faire passer tous les chats pour des sorciers.
All are not hunters who blow the horn. All are not cooks who sport white caps and carry long knives.

170 Le chat parti, les souris dansent.
When the cat's away, the mice will play.

171 Qui naquit chat court après les souris.
The son of a cat pursues the rat.

172 Un vieux chat aime les jeunes souris.
Old head and young hands. †Put an old cat to an old rat.

Chaumière   173 Chaumière où l'on rit vaut mieux que palais où l'on pleure.
Better little with content than much with contention.

Chaussure   174 Il n'y a aucune mauvaise chaussure qui ne trouve sa pareille.
There was never a shoe but had its mate.

Chemin   175 A chemin battu il ne croît point d'herbe.
Grass doesn't grow on a busy street.

176 Beau chemin n'est jamais long.
The right road is the shortest road.

177 Le chemin de fer et la marée n'attendent pas.
Time and tide wait for no man.

178 Les plus courts chemins ne sont pas toujours les meilleurs.
The longest road may be the quickest way home.
The shortcut is often the wrong cut.

179 Tous les chemins mènent à Rome.
All roads lead to Rome.

Cheminée   180 Nouvelle cheminée est bientôt enfumée.
The novelty of noon is out of date by night.

Chemise   181 La chemise (chair) est plus proche que le
               pourpoint (chemise).
               The shirt is nearer than the coat.

Chère   182 Grande chère, petit testament.
               Many estates are spent in getting.

Cheval   183 A bon cheval, bon gué.
               An old horse for a hard road.

               184 A cheval donné, ne lui regarde pas en la bouche.
               Don't look a gift horse in the mouth.

               185 A méchant cheval, bon éperon.
               A boisterous horse needs a rough bridle.

               186 Il est aisé d'aller à pied quand on tient son
               cheval par la bride.
               It is good walking with a horse in one's hand.

               187 Il fait toujours bon tenir son cheval par la bride.
               It is good to hold the ass by the bridle.

               188 Il ne faut pas changer un cheval borgne contre
               un aveugle.
               Better to be half blind than to have both eyes out.

               189 Il n'est si bon cheval qui ne bronche.
               It's a good horse that never stumbles.

               190 Qui veut un cheval sans défaut doit aller à pied.
               Better ride a poor horse than go afoot.

               191 Un bon cheval va bien tout seul à l'abreuvoir.
               The horse knows the way to its own stable.

Chevalier 192 Nul chevalier sans prouesse.
               Every man in his own way (after his fashion).

Chèvre

193 Où la chèvre est liée (atachée), il faut qu'elle broute.
The cow must graze where she is tied.

Chien

194 A bon chien bon os.
For a good dog, a good bone.

195 A méchant chien court lien.
A mischievous dog must be tied short. To a vicious dog, a short chain.

196 Autant vaut être mordu d'un chien que d'une chienne.
There's no choice among stinking fish.

197 Chien hargneux a toujours les oreilles déchirées.
A snappish dog usually has torn ears.
Quarreling dogs come halting home.

198 Chien sur son fumier est hardi.
Every dog is a lion at home (is brave in his own yard).

199 Comme le chien du jardinier qui ne mange pas des choux et ne veut pas que personne en mange.
Like the gardener's dog that neither eats cabbages himself, nor lets anybody else.

200 Il ne faut pas se moquer des chiens qu'on ne soit hors du village.
Do not halloo till you're out of the wood.

201 Jamais bon chien n'aboie à faux.
Dogs bark as they are bred.

202 Les chiens ne font pas des chats.
Eagles don't breed doves.

203 Mieux vaut chien vivant que lion mort.
Better a live dog than a dead lion.

204 Qui m'aime (aime Bertrand), aime mon (son) chien.
Love me, love my dog.

205 Qui se couche avec les chiens se lève avec des puces.
If you lie down with dogs, you'll get up with fleas.

206 Qui veut frapper un chien, facilement trouve un bâton.
He who has in mind to beat a dog will easily find a stick.

207 Qui veut tuer son chien l'accuse de la rage.
Give a dog an ill name and hang him.

208 Un chien mort ne mord pas.
Dead dogs never bite. *Dead men tell no tales.*

209 Un chien regarde bien un évêque.
A cat may look at a king.

Choisir

210 A force de choisir, on finit par se tromper.
He who has a choice, has trouble.

Chose

211 Chaque chose a son prix.
There is no good that does not cost a price.

212 Chaque chose a son temps.
Everything has its time.

213 Chose accoutumée rarement prisée.
The thing that often occurs is never much appreciated.

214 Chose bien commencée est à demi achevée.
Well begun is half done.

215 Chose défendue, chose désirée.
Everything forbidden is sweet. Forbid a thing and that we do.

216   Chose promise, chose due.
       A promise is a debt (*promise*).

217   En toute chose il faut considérer la fin.
       Look to the end. Think on the end before you begin.

218   Il ne faut pas mépriser (négliger) les petites
       choses.
       It's the little things in life that count.

219   La pire chose qui soit c'est une mauvaise femme.
       There's nothing better than a good woman and
       nothing worse than a bad one.

220   Plus on désire une chose, plus elle se fait attendre.
       Desires are nourished by delays.

221   Tant vaut la chose comme elle peut être vendue.
       The worth of a thing is what it will bring.

Chou   222   Ce n'est pas le tout que des choux, il faut le lard
       avec.
       There's more to riding than a pair of boots.

Clerc   223   Il ne faut pas parler latin devant les clercs.
       It is hard to sit in Rome and strive against the Pope.

224   Les plus grands clercs ne sont pas les plus fins.
       The greatest clerks are not always the wisest men.

Cloche   225   On ne peut sonner les cloches et aller à la
       procession.
       A man cannot whistle and eat a meal at the same
       time. The steam that blows the whistle will never
       turn the wheel.

226   Qui n'entend qu'une cloche n'entend qu'un son
       (n'entend rien).
       If you hear one bell only, you hear but one
       sound.

Clocher	227	Un grand clocher est un mauvais voisin. *The way is an ill neighbor. The best neighbours are vacant lots.*
Clou	228	Un clou chasse l'autre. One nail drives out another.
Coeur	229	De l'abondance du coeur, la bouche parle. *What the heart thinks, the tongue speaks.*
Colère	230	Colère n'a conseil. *Anger and haste hinder good counsel.*
Colombe	231	A colombes soûles, cerises sont amères. *When the cat is full, the milk tastes sour.*
	232	Craignez la colère de la colombe. *Beware the wrath of a patient man.*
Commence-ment	233	Heureux commencement est la moitié de l'oeuvre. A good beginning is half the task. Well begun, half done.
	234	Il y a un commencement à tout. Everything must have a beginning.
Compagnie	235	Il n'est si bonne compagnie qui ne se sépare (quitte). *The best of friends must part.*
	236	Les mauvaises compagnies corrompent les bonnes moeurs. Evil communications corrupt good manners.
	237	Par compagnie, on se fait pendre. *Some folks will go to Hell for company.*

Comparaison 238 Comparaison n'est pas raison.
No simile runs on all fours.

239 Toutes comparaisons sont odieuses.
Comparisons are odious.

Complaire 240 On ne peut complaire à tous.
You can't please everybody.

Compte 241 Les (bons) comptes courts font les (bons) amis longs.
Short accounts make long friends.

Condamner 242 Il ne faut pas condamner sans entendre.
No man should be condemned unheard.

Connaître 243 Pour connaître quelqu'un, il faut avoir mangé un minot de sel avec lui.
Before you make a friend, eat a peck of salt with him.

Conscience 244 Une bonne conscience est un bon oreiller.
A clean conscience is a good pillow.

Conseil 245 En conseil écoute le vieil.
If you wish good advice, consult an old man.

246 Les conseils de l'ennui sont les conseils du diable.
An idle brain is the devil's workshop.

247 Prends le premier conseil d'une femme et non le seconde.
Take the first advice of a woman and not the second.

Contentement 248 Contentement passe richesse.
Contentment is better than riches.

Convoiter	249	Qui tout convoite tout perd. All covet, all lose.
Convoitise	250	A convoitise rien ne suffit. Avarice is never satisfied.
Corbeau	251	Corbeaux avec corbeaux, ne se crèvent jamais les yeux. A crow does not pick out the eye of another crow.
	252	De mauvais corbeau mauvais oeuf. *Bad bird, bad eggs.*
	253	Elève (nourris) un corbeau, il te crévera les yeux. He has brought up a crow to pick out his own eyes.
	254	Jamais un corbeau n'a fait un canari. *A crow in a cage won't talk like a parrot.*
	255	Le jeune corbeau croasse à l'exemple du vieux. *As the old cock crows, so crows the young (the young one learns).*
	256	Qui lave un corbeau ne le fait pas blanc. A crow is no whiter for being washed.
Corde	257	Il ne faut point parler de corde dans la maison d'un pendu. Never talk of a rope in the house of a man who has been hanged.
Cordonnier	258	Les cordonniers sont toujours les plus mal chaussés. *All cobblers go barefoot. The cobbler's child is always the worst shod.*

Corsaire	259	A corsaire (renard)(trompeur)(vilain), corsaire (renard)(trompeur)(vilain) et demi. *Set a thief to catch a thief. It takes one to know one.*
Coupe	260	Il y a loin de la coupe aux lèvres (De la main à la bouche se perd souvent la coupe). *There's many a slip 'twixt the cup and the lip.*
Couteau	261	Qui frappe du couteau mourra de la gaine. *He that strikes by the sword, shall be beaten by the scabbard.*
Coutume	262	Coutume vainc droit. *Customs are stronger than laws.*
	263	Une fois n'est pas coutume. *One swallow does not make a summer. One flower makes no garland. †Once a use and ever a custom.*
Crédit	264	Crédit est mort, les mauvais payeurs l'ont tué. *Trust is dead, ill payment killed it.*
Critique	265	La critique est aisée, et l'art est dificile. *It's much easier to be critical than correct.*
Croire	266	Chacun croit aisément ce qu'il craint et ce qu'il désire. *We soon believe what we desire.*
Cruche	267	Tant va la cruche à l'eau qu'à la fin elle se brise (casse). *The pitcher that goes often to the well shall at last be broken.*

D

Danger   268 Au danger on connaît les braves.
Valour delights in the test. Calamity is the touchstone of a brave mind.

                    269 Danger passé, saint moqué.
Danger past, God is forgotten.

                    270 Il n'est danger que de vilain.
Art (science) has no enemy but ignorance.

Danser   271 Toujours va qui danse.
He who sings drives away his cares.

Défaut   272 Qui a le défaut a le soupçon.
Suspicion always haunts the guilty party. Who is in fault suspects everybody.

Défiance   273 La défiance est mère de sûreté.
Wise distrust is the parent of security.

Demain   274 Ne remets jamais à demain ce que tu peux faire aujourd'hui.
Never put off until tomorrow what you can do today.

Demande	275	A la folle (sotte) demande, point de réponse.

It is not every question that deserves an answer.
Silly question, silly answer.

Demander	276	Il n'en coûte rien de demander.

It costs nothing to ask.

277 Qui ne demande rien n'a rien.
He that cannot ask, cannot live.

Déménagement 278 Trois déménagements valent un incendie.
Three removes are as bad as a fire.

Dent 279 Bonnes sont les dents qui retiennent la langue.
Good that the teeth guard the tongue.

Dette 280 Qui paie ses dettes s'enrichit.
He who pays his debts enriches himself.
Out of debt is riches enough.

Deux 281 Jamais deux sans trois.
What happens twice happens thrice.

Devoir 282 On n'a jamais fini de faire son devoir.
A neglected duty returns tomorrow with seven others at its back.

Diable 283 Il n'est pas si diable qu'il est noir.
The devil is not as black as he is painted.

284 Le diable sait beaucoup parce qu'il est vieux.
The devil knows many things because he is old.

285 Quand le diable fut vieux, il se fit ermite.
Young devil, old angel.

Dieu

286   A toile ourdie, Dieu envoie le fil.
For a web begun God sends the thread.

287   Aide-toi, Dieu t'aidera.
God helps those who help themselves.

288   Dieu envoie le froid selon le drap.
God sends cold after clothes.

289   Il vaut mieux avoir affaire à Dieu qu'à ses saints.
When it pleases not God, the saint can do little.

290   Il y a un Dieu pour les ivrognes.
The devil places a pillow for a drunken man to fall on.

291   L'homme propose et Dieu dispose.
Man proposes, God disposes.

Différer

292   Ce qui est différé n'est pas perdu.
Delays are not denials.

Dire

293   Bien dire fait rire, bien faire fait taire.
Deeds will show themselves, and words will pass away. Doing is better than saying.

294   Du dire au fait, il y a long trait.
From word to deed is a great space.

Doigt

295   Il ne faut pas mettre le doigt entre l'arbre et l'écorce.
Put not your hand between the bark and the tree.

296   Tous les doigts de la main ne se ressemblent pas.
Every couple is not a pair.

Donner

297   Donner et retenir ne vaut.
Give a thing and take a thing, to wear the devil's gold ring.

298 Donner tard, c'est refuser.
To refuse and give tardily is all the same.

299 Qui tôt donne, deux fois donne.
He gives twice who gives quickly.

Douceur   300 Plus fait douceur que violence.
Kindness does more than violence.

Douleur   301 De toutes les douleurs on ne peut faire qu'une mort.
A man can die but once.

302 Les grandes douleurs sont muettes.
Who suffers much is silent.

Doute   303 Le doute est le commencement de la sagesse.
He who questions nothing learns nothing.

Douter   304 Qui doute ne se trompe pas.
He who believes easily is easily deceived.

Drap   305 On ne peut pas avoir le drap et l'argent.
You can't have your cake and eat it.

E

Eau	306	C'est folie puiser l'eau au cribleau. *Draw (carry) water in a sieve.*
	307	Chacun tire l'eau à son moulin. Every man draws water to his own mill.
	308	Il n'est pire eau que l'eau qui dort. *The stillest humours are always the worst.*
	309	L'eau trouble est le gain du pêcheur. *It is good fishing in troubled waters.*
	310	L'eau va toujours à la rivière. *The sea complains it wants water. He that has plenty of goods shall have more.*
Economiser	311	Qui économise s'enrichit. *Sparing is the first gaining. From saving comes having.*
Ecoute	312	Qui se tient aux écoutes entend souvent son fait. *Listen at the keyhole and you'll hear bad news about yourself. Listeners never hear good of themselves.*
Ecuelle	313	Qui s'attend à l'écuelle d'autrui est exposé à mal dîner. *He that lives on hope will have a slender diet.*

Effet 314 Les effets sont des mâles, les promesses sont des femelles.
Deeds are masculine, words are feminine.

Embrasser 315 Qui trop embrasse, mal étreint.
Grasp all, lose all.

Enfant 316 Enfants sont richesses de pauvres gens.
Children are poor men's riches.

317 Il n'y a plus d'enfants.
There are no children nowadays.

318 Les enfants sont ce qu'on les fait.
Parents are patterns.

319 Les hommes sont de grands enfants.
Men are but children of a larger growth.

320 Petits enfants - petite peine, grands enfants - grande peine.
Little children, little troubles; big children, big troubles.

Enfer 321 L'enfer est pavé de bonnes intentions.
Hell is paved with good intentions.

Ennemi 322 Il faut se défier d'un ennemi réconcilié.
Take heed of reconciled enemies.

323 Il n'est pire ennemi que ses proches.
Nothing worse than a familiar enemy.

324 Il n'y a pas de petit ennemi.
There is no little enemy.

325 Mieux vaut un sage ennemi qu'un sot ami.
A wise enemy is better than a foolish friend.

Entendeur	326	A bon entendeur demi-mot.
		A word to the wise is sufficient.
Envie	327	Envie passe avarice.
		Envy never enriched any man.
	328	Il vaut mieux faire envie que pitié.
		Better be envied than pitied.
Epargne	329	La plus belle épargne est celle du temps.
		He that gains time gains all things.
	330	L'épargne est un grand revenu.
		Sparing (thrift) is a great revenue.
Epée	331	Quiconque se sert de l'épée périra par l'épée.
		He who lives by the sword shall perish by the sword.
Espérance	332	L'espérance est le pain des malheureux.
		Hope is the poor man's bread.
	333	L'espérance est le songe d'un homme éveillé.
		Hope is but the dream of those that wake.
Esprit	334	Les beaux esprits se rencontrent.
		Great minds think alike.
Etincelle	335	Petite étincelle engendre grand feu.
		Of a small spark a great fire.
Etourneau	336	Les étourneaux sont maigres parce qu'ils vont en troupes.
		The smaller the company, the greater the feast.

Etre	337	Etre et paraître sont deux.
		Things are not always what they seem.
Evénement	338	Les grands événements procèdent des petites causes.
		From small beginnings come great things.
Exception	339	L'exception confirme la règle.
		The exception confirms the rule.
Excuser	340	Qui s'excuse s'accuse.
		He who excuses himself, accuses himself.
Expérience	341	Expérience est mère de science.
		Experience is the mother of science (knowledge)(wisdom).
	342	Expérience passe science.
		Experience without learning is better than learning without experience.
Extrême	343	Les extrêmes se touchent.
		Extremes meet.

F

Fâcher (se) 344 Qui se fâche a tort.
The weaker the argument, the stronger the words.

Fagot 345 Il y a fagots et fagots.
There may be blue and a better blue. There is some difference between Peter and Peter.

Faim 346 La faim chasse le loup hors du bois.
Hunger drives the wolf out of the wood.

347 La faim est une mauvaise conseillère.
An empty stomach is not a good political advisor.

Faire 348 Ce que l'on veut faire est plus beau que ce que l'on fait.
Many wants attend those who have many ambitions. The higher the aim, the higher the fall.

349 Ce qui est fait est fait.
What's done is done.

350 Ce qui est fait n'est plus à faire.
The thing that's done is not to do.

351 Fais ce que je dis et non ce que je fais.
Do as I say, not as I do.

352 Qui ne fait pas quand il peut, ne fait pas quand il veut.
He that will not when he may, when he will he shall have nay.

Familiarité 353 La familiarité engendre le mépris.
Familiarity breeds contempt.

Fantaisie 354 La fantaisie (caprice) fait la loi à la raison.
Imagination rules the world.

Fatigue 355 La fatigue du corps est la santé de l'âme.
A strong body makes the mind strong.

Faute 356 Faute avouée est à demi pardonnée.
A fault confessed is half-redressed.

Faux 357 Il ne faut pas jeter la faux en la moisson d'autrui.
Don't thrust your sickle in another's corn.
Hoe your own row.

Femme 358 Beauté de femme n'enrichit l'homme.
Beauty is no inheritance.

359 Ce que femme veut, Dieu le veut.
Women will have their wills.

360 Femme bonne vaut une couronne.
A virtuous woman is rarer than a precious jewel.
A worthy woman is the crown of her husband.

361 Femme rit quand elle peut et pleure quand elle veut.
A woman laughs when she can and weeps when she pleases.

362 Il faut chercher une femme avec les oreilles
     plutôt qu'avec les yeux.
     Choose a wife by your ear rather than by your
     eye.

363 La femme est la clef du ménage.
     The wife is the key of the house.

364 Qui femme a, guerre a (noise a).
     He that has a wife, has strife.

365 Trois femmes font un marché.
     Three women make a market.

Fer

366 Il faut battre le fer pendant qu'il est chaud.
     Strike while the iron is hot.

Ferveur

367 Il n'est ferveur que de novice.
     A new broom sweeps clean.

Fête

368 Il ne faut chômer les fêtes avant qu'elles soient
     venues.
     *Do not triumph before the victory. Gut no fish till
     you get them.*

369 Il n'est pas tous les jours fête (noces).
     Every day is not a holiday.

370 Il n'y a point de bonne fête sans lendemain.
     Drunken days have all their tomorrows.

371 La fête passée, adieu le saint.
     Danger (river) past, God is forgotten.

Feuille

372 Qui a peur des feuilles, ne va point au bois.
     He that fears leaves must not come into a wood.

Fille

373 La plus belle fille du monde ne peut donner que ce qu'elle a.
No one can give what he has not got.

374 Quand la fille est mariée, on trouve toujours des gendres.
When the child is christened, you may have godfathers enough. No use locking the stable door once the horse has bolted. After meat, mustard.

Fils

375 Chacun est le fils de ses oeuvres.
Every man is the son of his own works.

Fin

376 Fin contre fin ne vaut rien pour doublure.
Hard with hard makes not the stone wall.

377 La fin couronne l'oeuvre.
The end crowns the work.

378 La fin justifie les moyens. (Qui veut la fin veut les moyens.)
The end justifies the means.

Fleur

379 Qui peint la fleur n'en peut peindre l'odeur.
Painted flowers have no scent.

Folie

380 C'est folie de faire de son médecin son héritier.
He is a fool that makes his doctor his heir.

Fontaine

381 Il ne faut jamais dire: fontaine, je ne boirai pas de ton eau.
Never say never.

Force

382 Force n'est pas droit.
Might is not right.

Forgeron	383	C'est en forgeant qu'on devient forgeron. *Practice makes perfect. In doing we learn.*
Fortune	384	Bien danse à qui la fortune chante. *He dances well to whom fortune pipes.*
	385	De fortune et de santé il ne faut jamais se vanter. *Do not cry roast meat.*
	386	Grande fortune, grande servitude. *A man of wealth is a slave to his possessions.*
	387	La fortune rit aux sots. *Fortune favours fools.*
Fossé	388	Au bout du fossé, la culbute. *They that dance must pay the fiddler. Merry is the feast-making till we come to the reckoning.*
Fou	389	A chaque fou sa marotte. *Every man is mad on some point.*
	390	Fou qui se tait passe pour sage. *A fool who is silent is counted wise. Fools are wise as long as silent.*
	391	Il n'est si sage qui ne foloie. *No man is wise at all times.*
	392	Il n'y a que les fous qui ne changent pas d'avis. *A fool never changes his mind, but a wise man does.*
	393	Il vaut mieux être fou avec tous que sage tout seul. *Better to be a fool with a crowd than a wise man by oneself.*
	394	Les fous font les fêtes, les sages en ont le plaisir. *Fools make feasts, and wise men eat them.*

395 Les fous inventent les modes, les sages les suivent.
Fools may invent fashions that wise men will
wear.

Four   **396** Le four appelle le moulin «brulé».
Ill may the kiln call the oven burnt-tail.
The pot calls the kettle black.

397 On ne peut être à la fois au four et au moulin.
A man cannot whistle and eat a meal (be in two
places) at the same time.

Fréquenter   **398** Dis-moi qui tu fréquentes (hantes) et je te dirai
qui tu es.
Show me your companions and I'll tell you who
you are.
Tell me with whom you go, and I'll tell what you
do.

Frotter   **399** Qui s'y frotte, s'y pique.
He that sows thistles, shall reap prickles.

Fumée   **400** Il n'y a pas (point) de fumée sans feu.
There's no smoke without a fire.

G

Gardon   401 Jeter un gardon pour avoir un brochet.
                        Throw out a sprat to catch a mackerel.

Génie   402 Il n'y a point de génie sans un grain de folie.
                        Genius is akin to madness.

                  403 Le génie est une longue patience.
                        Genius is the capacity for taking infinite pains.

Gloire   404 Quand vient la gloire, s'en va la mémoire.
                        When glory comes, memory departs.

Gourmand   405 Gourmands font leur fosses avec leurs dents.
                        Greedy eaters dig their graves with their teeth.

Goût   406 Des goûts et des couleurs, on ne discute pas.
                        There is no disputing concerning tastes.

                  407 Tous les goûts sont dans la nature.
                        There is no accounting for taste(s).

Goutte   408 Goutte à goutte l'eau creuse la pierre.
                        The constant drop (dripping) wears away the
                        stone.

Gourmandise	409	La gourmandise tue plus de gens que l'épée. Gluttony kills more than the sword.
Gouvernement	410	Toute nation a le gouvernement qu'elle mérite. People get the government they deserve.
Grain	411	De mauvais grain jamais bon pain. *Of evil grain no good seed can come.*
	412	Grain à grain la poule remplit son ventre. Grain by grain, and the hen fills her belly.
	413	Qui sème bon grain recueille bon pain. *He that sows good seed, shall reap good corn.*
Grive	414	Faute de grives, on mange des merles. *If you have not a capon, feed on an onion. What they want in meat, let them take out in drink.*
Gué	415	Il ne faut pas louer le gué avant de l'avoir passé. It is no good praising a ford till a man be over.
Guérison	416	La guérison n'est jamais si prompte que la blessure. One is not so soon healed as hurt.
Guerre	417	A la guerre comme à la guerre. *Take the rough with the smooth.*
	418	Il ne faut pas aller à la guerre qui craint horions. He that is afraid of wounds must not come near a battle.
	419	Si tu veux la paix, prépare (tiens-toi prêt à faire) la guerre. If you desire peace, prepare for war.

H

Habit	420	L'habit ne fait pas le moine. The habit (cowl) does not make the monk.
	421	L'habit volé ne va pas au voleur. *Stolen goods never thrive.*
	422	Tout habit sied bien à qui en a besoin. *When in great need, anything will do.* *All's good in a famine.*
Habitude	423	L'habitude est une seconde nature. Custom (habit) is second nature.
Hâte	424	Qui se marie à la hâte se repent à loisir. Marry in haste and repent at leisure.
Herbe	425	Mauvaise herbe croît toujours. Ill weeds grow apace. *Weeds want no sowing.*
Héros	426	Il n'y a point de héros (grand homme) pour son valet de chambre. No man is a hero to his valet.
Heureux	427	Est heureux qui croit l'être. *No man is ever happy unless he thinks himself so.*

Heurter	428	On se heurte toujours où l'on a mal.
		Bread never falls but on its buttered side.
Hirondelle	429	Une hirondelle ne fait pas le printemps.
		One swallow does not make a spring.
Homme	430	A un pauvre homme sa vache meurt et au riche son enfant.
		A poor man's cow dies, a rich man's child.
	431	A vaillant homme, courte épée.
		A brave arm makes a short sword long.
	432	D'un petit homme souvent grand ombre.
		Don't measure your importance by your morning shadow.
	433	Il ne faut pas louer un homme avant sa mort.
		Praise no man till he is dead.
	434	L'homme ne vit pas seulement de pain.
		Man cannot live by bread alone.
	435	Pauvre homme n'a pas d'amis.
		A poor man has no friends.
	436	Quand l'homme perd son esprit, il perd tous ses moyens.
		What is a man but his mind? The mind of the man is the man.
	437	Riche homme ne sait qui lui est ami.
		The rich knows not who is his friend.
	438	Un homme averti en vaut deux.
		Forewarned is forearmed.
	439	Un homme mort n'a ni parents ni amis.
		Dead men are of no family, and are akin to none.
	440	Un homme qui se noie s'accroche à tout.
		A drowning man will catch at a straw.

Honneur	441	Honneur perdu ne se retrouve plus. *A broken reputation is never mended.*
	442	Les honneurs changent les moeurs. Honours change manners.
	443	Mieux vaut trésor d'honneur que d'or. *A good name is better than gold.*
Honni	444	Honni soit qui mal y pense. Evil be to him who evil thinks.
Honte	445	Qui a honte de manger a honte de vivre. *A good eater is a happy man.*
Honteux	446	Jamais honteux n'eut belle amie. Faint heart never won fair lady.
	447	Il n'y a que des honteux qui perdent. He who hesitates is lost.
Hôte	448	L'hôte et la pluie après trois jours ennuient. *Fish and guests (visitors) smell in three days.*
	449	Qui compte sans hôte compte deux fois. He that reckons without his host must reckon again.
Huile	450	Il ne faut pas jeter de l'huile sur le feu. *To pour oil on the fire is not the way to quench it.*
	451	L'huile et vérité finissent par être au sommet. Truth and oil always come to the top (are ever above).

I

Ignorance	452	Ignorance est mère de tous les vices.
		Ignorance is the father of crime. Ignorance is the mother of conceit (devotion) (impudence) (superstition).
Impossible	453	A l'impossible, nul n'est tenu.
		No one is bound to do the impossible.
Inattention	454	L'inattention fait échouer le navire.
		A forgotten switch may cause a wreck.
Injure	455	Les injures s'écrivent sur l'airain et les bienfaits sur le sable.
		Injuries are written in brass.
		†*Write injuries in dust, benefits (kindness) in marble.*
	456	Les injures sont les raisons de ceux qui ont tort.
		The weaker the argument, the stronger the words.

J

Jaunisse   457 Qui a la jaunisse, voit tout jaune.
                        To the jaundiced eye, all things look yellow.

Jeu   458 A beau jeu, beau retour.
                        One good turn deserves another. Give as good as
                        one gets.

                   459 Heureux au jeu, malheureux en amour.
                        Lucky at play, unlucky in love.

                   460 Le jeu ne vaut pas la chandelle.
                        The game is not worth the candle.

                   461 Qui en jeu entre, jeu consente.
                        He who plays with a cat must expect to be scratched.

Jeunesse   462 Il faut travailler en jeunesse pour reposer en
                        vieillesse.
                        Application in youth makes old age comfortable.

                   463 Jeunesse oiseuse, vieillesse disetteuse.
                        An idle youth, a needy age.

                   464 Jeunesse rêve, vieillesse décompte.
                        A young man looks into the future as an old man
                        into his past.

                   465 Si jeunesse savait, si vieillesse pouvait.
                        If youth but knew and age but could (do).

Joie	466	Joie au coeur fait beau teint. A blithe heart makes a blooming visage. A merry heart makes a cheerful countenance.
	467	L'on doit avoir joie du bien à son voisin. *Never rejoice about your neighbour's misfortunes.*
Joueur	468	(La balle cherche le joueur) A bon joueur la balle lui vient. The ball comes to the player.
Jour	469	A chaque jour suffit sa peine (son mal). Sufficient unto each day is the evil thereof.
	470	Il n'y a si long jour qui ne vienne à la nuit. Long as the day may be, the night comes at last.
	471	Il y a encore des jours après aujourd'hui. *Tomorrow is another day.*
	472	Loue le beau jour au soir, et la vie à la mort. *Praise a fine day at night.*
Juge	473	De fou juge, briève sentence. From a foolish judge, a quick sentence.
	474	On ne peut être à la fois juge et partie. No man ought to be judge in his own cause.
Justice	475	L'extrême justice est une extrême injure. Extreme justice (law)(right) is extreme injustice (wrong)(injury).
	476	On aime la justice dans la maison d'autrui. *We all love justice - at our neighbour's expense.*

L

Laine   477 Il vaut mieux donner la laine que le mouton.
                    Better give the wool than the sheep.

Langue   478 Beau parler n'écorche pas la langue.
                    Fair words hurt not the tongue (mouth).

               479 La langue va où la dent fait mal.
                    The tongue returns to the aching tooth.

               480 Langue de miel, coeur de fiel.
                    A honey tongue, a heart of gall.

               481 Longue langue, courte main.
                    A long tongue has a short hand.

Lard   482 On ne peut avoir le lard et le cochon.
                    You cannot have the cake and eat it. You cannot
                    sell the cow and sup the milk.

Larme   483 Rien ne sèche plus vite que les larmes.
                    Nothing dries sooner than tears.

Larron   484 Les gros larrons font pendre les petits.
                    The big thieves hang the little thieves.

               485 L'occasion fait le larron.
                    Opportunity makes a thief.

Lévrier

486 De toutes tailles bons lévriers.
No good horse of a bad colour.

Lièvre

487 Ce n'est pas toujours celui qui lève le lièvre qui le prend.
One beats the bush and another catches the birds.

488 Il ne faut pas courir deux lièvres à la fois (Qui court deux lièvres à la fois n'en prend aucun). He who chases two hares catches neither.

489 Le lièvre retourne toujours à son gite.
The hare always returns to her form.

490 On n'attrape pas de lièvre avec un tambour.
A hare is not caught with a drum.

491 Mieux vaut un lièvre pris que trois en liberté.
A bird in the hand is worth two in the bush.

Lime

492 Au long aller la lime mange le fer.
Time is a file that wears and makes no noise.

Linceul

493 Le plus riche (en mourant) n'emporte qu'un linceul (drap).
Shrouds have no pockets.

Linge

494 Il faut laver son linge sale en famille.
Wash your dirty linen at home.

Lisière

495 La lisière est pire que le drap.
There's no wedge worse than one from the same log.

Lit

496 Comme on fait son lit, on se couche.
As one makes his bed, so must he lie.

Livre	497	Gardez-vous de l'homme qui ne connaît qu'un livre. Beware of the man of one book.
Loup	498	A chair de loup, sauce de chien. *What's sauce for the goose is sauce for the gander.*
	499	Avec les loups on apprend à hurler. Who keeps company with a wolf learns to howl.
	500	Il ne faut pas mettre le loup berger. Don't set a wolf to watch the sheep.
	501	Le loup (renard) change de poil, mais non de naturel. The wolf may lose his teeth, but never his nature. †*A wolf may change his mind but not his fur.*
	502	Le loup est toujours loup. *Once a thief, always a thief.*
	503	Les loups ne se mangent pas entre eux. Wolves never prey upon wolves.
	504	On fait toujours le loup plus gros qu'il n'est. *The devil is not as black as he is painted.*
	505	Quand le loup est pris, tous les chiens lui lardent (mordent) les fesses. *When a man is down, everyone runs over him.*
	506	Quand on parle du loup, on en voit la queue. *Talk of the devil and he is sure to appear. Talk of angels and you will hear the flutter of their wings.*
Lune	507	La lune est à l'abri des loups. *The moon does not heed the barking of wolves (dogs).*

M

Magnificat   508 Il ne faut pas chanter le magnificat à matines.
                       *Don't sing triumph before you have conquere*d.

Main   509 Froides mains, chaudes amours.
                       A cold hand, a warm heart.

                  510 Les mains noires font manger le pain blanc.
                       Dirty hands make clean money.

Maison   511 Chétive est la maison où le coq se tait et la poule
                       chante.
                       It is a sad house where the hen crows louder
                       than the cock.

                  512 Grandes maisons se font par petite cuisine.
                       A little kitchen makes a large house.

                  513 Les maisons empêchent de voir la ville.
                       You cannot see the city for the houses.

Maître   514 Il n'y a si fort qui ne trouve son maître.
                       Everyone has his master.

                  515 Les bons maîtres font les bons valets.
                       A bad master makes a bad servant.

                  516 Nul ne peut servir deux maîtres à la fois.
                       No man can serve two masters.

517 Tel maître, tel valet.
Like master, like man.

518 Voyages de maîtres, noces de valet.
When the cat's away the mice will play.

Mal

519 Aux grands maux les grands remèdes.
Desperate evils require desperate remedies.

520 Chacun sent son mal.
Everyone thinks his sack heaviest.

521 De bien faire grand mal vient.
Kind hearts are soonest wronged.

522 Il n'y aucun mal qui ne serve à quelque bien.
There is nothing so bad in which there is not
something good.

523 Le mal (les maladies) vient (viennent) à cheval et
s'en retourne(nt) à pied.
Misfortune arrives on horseback but departs on
foot.

524 Mal d'autrui n'est que songe.
We can always bear our neighbours' misfortune.

525 Qui mal cherche mal trouve.
He that seeks trouble never misses.

Malheur

526 A quelque chose malheur est bon.
Ill luck is good for something.

527 Assez gagne qui malheur perd.
He gains enough whom fortune loses.

528 Le malheur des uns fait le bonheur des autres.
The folly of one man is the fortune of another.

529 Malheur se plaît à la surprise.
Trouble arises when you least expect it.

530 Un malheur n'arrive jamais seul.
Misfortunes (misery) never (seldom) come(s) alone (singly).

Manche 531 Il ne faut pas jeter la manche après la cognée.
Do not throw the helve after the hatchet.

Manteau 532 Quand il fait beau, prends ton manteau; quand il pleut, prends-le si tu veux.
Though the sun shines, leave not your cloak at home.

Marchand 533 Marchand d'oignons se connaît en ciboulettes.
Everyone knows his own business best.

Marchandise 534 Il ne faut pas juger la marchandise par l'étiquette du sac.
Don't judge a book by its cover.

Marché 535 Bon marché ruine.
Good cheap is dear.

536 On n'a jamais bon marché de mauvaise marchandise.
Ill ware is never cheap.

537 On vend au marché plus de harengs que de soles.
Fish for herring and catch sprat.

Mariage 538 Les mariages sont écrits dans le ciel.
Marriages are made in heaven.

Matin 539 Qui rit le matin le soir pleure.
Laugh before breakfast, cry before sunset (supper).

Matinée   540   Qui dort grasse matinée, trotte toute la journée.
He that rises late, trots all day.

Médaille   541   Toute médaille a son revers.
Every medal has its reverse.

Médecin   542   De jeune médecin cimetière bossu.
A young physician should have three graveyards.

543   Les fautes du médecin, la terre les recouvre.
The doctor's faults are covered with earth.

544   Médecin, guéris-toi toi-même.
Physician, heal thyself.

Meilleur   545   Le meilleur est toujours le moins cher.
The best is cheapest (in the end).

Mémoire   546   Qui n'a pas de mémoire doit avoir des jambes.
What your head forgets, your feet must remember.

Ménétrier   547   En la maison du ménétrier chacun est danseur.
In the house of a fiddler, all fiddle.

Mensonge   548   Qui dit un mensonge, en dit cent.
One lie makes many.

Menteur   549   A menteur, menteur et demi.
It takes a liar to call someone a liar. You can't kid a kidder.

550   Il faut qu'un menteur ait bonne mémoire (A bon mensonge, longue mémoire).
A liar should have a good memory.

551   On attrape plus vite un menteur qu'un voleur.
A liar is sooner caught than the cripple.

552 Un menteur n'est point écouté, même en disant
la vérité.
A liar is not believed when he speaks the truth.

Mentir 553 A beau mentir qui vient de loin.
A traveller may lie with authority.

Mercier 554 A petit mercier, petit panier.
A small pack becomes a small peddlar.

Mère 555 La bonne mère ne dit pas: veux-tu?
The good mother says not, "Will you?" but gives.

556 Telle mère, telle fille.
Like mother, like daughter.

Mérite 557 Mérite d'abord et puis demande.
First deserve and then desire.

Merle 558 On ne prend pas les vieux merles à la pipée.
You cannot catch old birds with chaff.

Métier 559 Chacun son métier.
Every man to his trade.

560 Il n'est point de sot métier.
All work is noble.

561 Qui a métier, a rente.
Who has a trade, has a share everywhere.

Miel 562 Le miel est doux mais l'abeille pique.
Honey is sweet, but bees sting.

563 Nul miel sans fiel.
Every sweet has its bitter.

564   Trop achète le miel qui sur épine le lèche.
Don't lick the honey off a briar even if it is sweet.

Mieux   565   Le mieux est l'ennemi du bien.
Best is often the enemy of the good.

Misère   566   Misère et pauvreté font mauvais ménage.
When poverty comes in at the door, love flies out the window.

Moelle   567   Pour avoir la moelle, il faut briser l'os.
He who does not kill hogs will not get black puddings.

Moine   568   Le moine répond comme l'abbaye chante.
Such is the priest, such is the clerk. As the old cock crows, the young cock learns.

Moineau   569   Deux moineaux sur un même épi ne sont pas longtemps unis.
Two sparrows on one ear of corn make an ill agreement.

570   Moineau en main vaut mieux que perdrix qui vole.
Better a sparrow in the hand than a pigeon on the roof.

Monde   571   On ne peut contenter tout le monde et son père.
You can't please the whole world and his wife.

Monnaie   572   Monnaie fait tout.
Money will do everything (anything).

Montagne   573 Il n'y a que les montagnes qui ne se rencontrent
                     jamais.
                     Two men may meet, but mountains never.

                574 Nulle montagne sans vallée.
                     There is no hill without a valley.

Monter   575 Celui qui monte haut de haut tombe. (De
                     grande montée, grande chute.)
                     The higher they climb, the lower they fall.
                     (Climb not too high lest the fall be greater.)

Monture   576 Qui veut voyager loin ménage sa monture.
                     He who wants to travel far saves his horse.

Mort   577 Après la mort, le médecin.
                     After death, the doctor.

                578 La mort a toujours tort. (Les morts ont tort.)
                     The dead are always wrong.

                579 On ne doit appeler personne heureux avant sa
                     mort.
                     Call no man happy till he is dead.

                580 Rien n'est plus certain que la mort, rien n'est
                     plus incertain que l'heure de la mort.
                     *No man knows when he shall die, although he
                     knows he must die.*

Morveux   581 Il vaut mieux laisser son enfant morveux que de
                     lui arracher le nez.
                     Better a snotty child than his nose wiped off.

                582 Les morveux veulent moucher les autres.
                     The pot calls the kettle black.

                583 Qui se sent morveux se mouche.
                     If the cap fits, wear it.

Mot   584 Qui ne dit mot consent.
                     Silence gives consent.

Mouche   585 On prend (attrape) plus de mouches avec du
                     miel qu'avec du vinaigre.
                     Honey catches more flies than vinegar.

Moulin   586 Il faut faire tourner le moulin lorsque le vent
                     souffle.
                     The mill cannot grind with water that is past.

                 587 Qui premier vient au moulin premier doit
                     moudre.
                     First come, first served.

Mur   588 C'est au pied du mur qu'on voit le maçon.
                     It is working that makes a workman.

                 589 Les murs ont des oreilles.
                     Walls have ears.

Mule   590 La mule du pape ne mange qu'à ses heures.
                     The ass loaded with gold still eats thistles.

Mûre   591 On ne va pas aux mûres sans crochet.
                     Don't hunt with unwilling hounds.

N

Nageur 592 Bons nageurs sont à la fin noyés.
Good swimmers at length are drowned.

Nature 593 Nature ne peut mentir.
Interest will not lie.

Naturel 594 Chassez le naturel, il revient au galop.
What is bred in the bone will come out in the flesh.

Navire 595 A navire brisé tous vents sont contraires.
Every wind is ill to a broken ship.

596 Le navire qui n'obéit pas au gouvernail devra bien obéir au récif.
The vessel that will not obey her helm will have to obey the rocks.

Nécessité 597 Il faut faire de nécessité vertu.
Make a virtue of necessity.

598 Nécessité est mère d'invention (industrie).
Necessity is the mother of invention.

599 Nécessité fait trotter les vieilles.
Need makes the old wife trot.

600 Nécessité n'a pas (point) de loi.
Necessity knows no law.

Nenni   601 Dites toujours nenni, vous ne serez jamais marié.
                        If you always say «no» you'll never be married.

Nez   602 Un grand nez ne gâte jamais beau visage.
                        A big nose never spoiled a handsome face.

Noeud   603 On ne peut faire un gros noeud sur une petite
                        corde.
                        *A great shoe fits not a little foot. With small men
                        no great thing can be accomplished.*

Noix   604 Pour manger la noix, il faut casser la coque.
                        He that would eat the kernel must crack the nut.

                   605 Qui a des noix, en casse; qui n'en a pas, s'en
                        passe.
                        A wise man cares not for what he cannot have.

Nouveau   606 Au nouveau tout est beau.
                        Everything new is fine.

                   607 Rien de nouveau sous le soleil.
                        Nothing new under the sun.

Nouvelles   608 Les mauvaises nouvelles ont des ailes.
                        Bad news travels fast.

                   609 Pas de nouvelles, bonnes nouvelles.
                        No news is good news.

Nuire   610 Ce qui nuit à l'un sert à l'autre.
                        What is good for one man may not be good for
                        another.

Nuit   611 Attendez à la nuit pour dire que le jour a été bon.
                        Praise a fair day at night.

612 La nuit porte conseil.
     Night is the mother of counsel.
     The best advice is found on the pillow.

613 La nuit, tous les chats sont gris.
     All dogs are grey in the night.

O

Obéir   614   Qui ne sait obéir ne sait commander.
If you wish to command, learn to obey.

Obéissance   615   L'obéissance vaut mieux que tous les sacrifices.
Obedience is better than sacrifice.

Observer   616   Qui n'observe rien n'apprend rien.
In order to learn, we must attend.

Occasion   617   Il faut saisir l'occasion aux cheveux.
Take opportunity by the forelock.

Oeil   618   Il vaut mieux se fier à ses yeux qu'à ses oreilles.
It is better to trust the eye than the ear.

             619   Les yeux sont le miroir de l'âme.
The eyes are the mirror (window) of the soul.

             620   L'oeil du maître engraisse le cheval.
The master's eye makes the horse fat.

             621   Loin des yeux, loin du coeur.
Out of sight, out of mind.

             622   Oeil pour oeil, dent pour dent.
An eye for an eye, a tooth for a tooth.

623 Quand on a mal aux yeux, il n'y faut toucher
que du coude.
Never rub your eye but with your elbow.

624 Quatre (deux) yeux voient mieux (plus claire)
que deux (qu'un).
Four eyes see more than two.

Oeuf

625 Il ne faut mettre tous ses oeufs dans un même
panier.
Don't put all your eggs in one basket.

626 Qui vole un oeuf vole un boeuf.
He that steals an egg will steal a chicken.

627 Un oeuf aujourd'hui vaut mieux qu'un poulet
pour demain. (Mieux vaut promptement un oeuf
que demain un boeuf.)
Better an egg today than a hen tomorrow.

628 Veux-tu des oeufs, souffre le caquetage des poules.
He that would have eggs must endure the cak-
ling of hens.

Offenseur

629 L'offenseur ne pardonne pas.
The offender never pardons.

Oiseau

630 A chaque oiseau son nid est beau.
Every bird likes his own nest best.

631 A petit oiseau, petit nid.
Little bird, little nest.

632 Au chant on connaît l'oiseau.
A bird is known by his note.

633 L'oiseau ne vole pas sur sa gorge.
Fed hounds don't hunt.

634 Petit à petit l'oiseau fait son nid.
Little by little the bird builds his nest.

635 Plus l'oiseau est vieux, moins il veut se défaire de
sa plume.
The older the bird, the more unwillingly it parts
with its feathers.

636 Un oiseau dans la main vaut mieux que deux
dans la haie.
A bird in the hand is worth two in the bush.

637 Vilain oiseau que celui qui salit son lit.
It's an ill bird that fowls its own nest.

Oisiveté

638 L'oisiveté est la mère de tous les vices.
Idleness is the mother of all the vices.

Omelette

639 On ne fait pas d'omelette sans casser d'oeufs
You cannot make an omelette without breaking
eggs.

Once

640 Mieux vaut une once de fortune qu'une livre de
sagesse.
A pocketful of luck is worth a sackful of wisdom.

641 Une once de bon esprit vaut mieux qu'une livre
de science.
A handful of common sense is worth a bushel of
learning.
An ounce of wisdom is worth a pound of wit.

642 Une once de bonne réputation vaut mieux que
mille livres d'or.
A good reputation is more valuable than money.
A good name is better than riches.

Ongle

643 A l'ongle on connaît le lion.
The lion is known by his claws.

Or	644	Nul or sans écume. No gold (silver) without its dross.
	645	Or, ami, vin, serviteur, le plus vieux est le meilleur. *Old friends and old wine and old gold are best.*
	646	Tout ce qui brille (reluit) n'est pas or. All that glitters is not gold.
Orage	647	Toujours ne dure orage ni guerre. *Nothing that is violent is permanent. Nothing lasts forever.*
Ordure	648	Plus on remue l'ordure, plus elle pue. The more you stir dirt, the more it stinks.
Orgueil	649	L'orgueil précède les chutes. Pride goes before a fall.
	650	Lorsque orgueil va devant, honte et dommage le suivent. *Pride goes before, and shame follows after.*
Ouvrage	651	A l'ouvrage connaît-on l'ouvrier (A l'oeuvre on connaît l'artisan). The workman is known by his work.
Ouvrier	652	Il est plus d'ouvriers que de maîtres. Workmen are easier found than masters.
	653	Mauvais ouvrier ne trouve jamais bon outil. A bad workman always blames his tools. *A bad shearer never had a good sickle.*
	654	Tout ouvrier est digne de son salaire. (Un bon ouvrier n'est jamais trop chèrement payé.) A workman is worthy of his hire.

P

Paille

655 Un noyé s'accroche à un brin de paille.
A drowning man will catch at a straw.

Pain

656 Le pain d'autrui est amer.
Bitter is the bread of charity.

Paix

657 Qui de tout se tait de tout a paix.
The tree of silence bears the fruit of peace.

Papier

658 Le papier souffre tout.
Paper is patient *(does not blush)*.

Parents

659 Nous sommes tous parents en Adam.
We are all Adam's children.

Paresseux

660 Le paresseux est frère du mendiant.
The slothful man is the beggar's brother.
Idleness is the key of beggary.

Paris

661 Qui se tient à Paris ne sera jamais pape.
He that stays in the valley shall never get over the hill.

662 Parler sans penser, c'est tirer sans gagner.
Speaking without thinking is shooting without aiming.

Parler	663	Qui parle sème, qui écoute récolte.
		He that speaks sows, and he that holds his peace gathers.
Paroisse	664	Chacun prêche pour sa paroisse.
		Everyone speaks for his own interest.
Parole	665	La parole est d'argent, le silence est d'or.
		Speech is silver, silence is golden.
	666	Les paroles sont femmes, et les écrits sont hommes.
		Words are feminine, deeds are masculine.
	667	Les belles paroles ne donnent pas à manger.
		Fair words fill not the belly (butter no parsnips) (won't make the pot boil).
Partie	668	Il ne faut pas remettre la partie au lendemain.
		Don't put off for tomorrow what you can do today.
Partir	669	Partir, c'est mourir un peu.
		Parting is such sweet sorrow.
Pas	670	Ce n'est pas pour un mauvais pas qu'on tue un boeuf.
		Don't muzzle the ox when he treads out the corn.
	671	Il n'y a que le premier pas qui coûte.
		It's the first step that costs (counts).
	672	Pas à pas on va bien loin.
		Step by step, one goes a long way.
Patience	673	La patience est amère, mais son fruit est doux.
		Patience is bitter, but its root is sweet.

674 La patience vient à bout de tout.
Patience conquers.
Patience is a remedy for every grief.

675 Patience passe science.
Patience surpasses learning.

Pâture

676 Changement de pâture réjouit les (donne appétit aux) veaux.
Change of pasture makes fat calves.

Pauvre

677 La main du pauvre est la bourse de Dieu.
He who gives to the poor, lends to God.

678 N'est pauvre qui a peu, mais qui désire beaucoup.
He is not poor that has little, but he that desires more.

Pauvreté

679 Pauvreté n'est pas vice.
Poverty is no crime (sin) (shame).

680 Quand la pauvreté entre par la porte, amour s'en va par la fenêtre.
When poverty comes in at the door, love goes out the window.

Peau

681 Dans sa peau mourra le loup (renard).
The wolf must die in his own skin.

682 Il faut coudre la peau du renard à celle du lion.
If the lion's skin cannot, the fox's shall.

683 Il ne faut vendre la peau de l'ours avant de l'avoir tué.
To sell the bear's skin before one has caught the bear.

Péché

684 Péché caché est à demi pardonné.
Sin that is hidden is half-forgiven.

Pêcher	685	Toujours pêche qui en prend un.
		Still he fishes that catches one.

Peigne   686   Jamais teigneux n'aima le peigne.
Never comb a bald head.

Peine   687   Ce qui vaut la peine d'être fait vaut la peine
d'être bien fait.
What is worth doing at all is worth doing well.

688   La peine et le plaisir se suivent.
Sadness and gladness succeed each other.

Pensée   689   Les pensées ne paient point de douane.
Thought is free.

Penser   690   Mal pense qui ne repense.
He thinks not well that thinks not again.
Second thoughts are best.

Perdre   691   Nul ne perd qu'autrui ne gagne.
One man's loss is another man's gain.

692   On risque de tout perdre en voulant trop gagner.
All covet, all lose. Covetousness breaks the sack.

693   Pour un perdu, deux retrouvés.
What we lose in hake we shall have in herring.

Père   694   Un père peut nourrir cent enfants mais cent
enfants ne nourissent pas un père.
*One father is enough to govern one hundred sons,
but not a hundred sons one father.*

Personne   695   Ce que trois personnes savent est public.
It is no secret that is known to three.

Petit   696 Mieux vaut petit mais de longue durée.
                    Better a little along than a long none.

Pied   697 Autant fait celui qui tient le pied que celui qui
                    écorche.
                    He who holds the ladder is as bad as the thief.

               698 Il vaut mieux glisser du pied que de la langue.
                    Better the foot slip than the tongue.

Pierre   699 Déshabiller Saint Pierre pour habiller Saint Paul.
                    Rob Peter to pay Paul.

               700 La pierre va toujours au tas.
                    No stone ever falls alone.
                    It never rains but it pours.

               701 Pierre qui roule n'amasse pas mousse.
                    †The rolling stone gathers no moss.*

Pigeon   702 Il ne faut pas laisser de semer par crainte des
                    pigeons.
                    Forbear not sowing because of birds.

Plaisir   703 Chacun prend son plaisir où il le trouve.
                    Happiness is where you find it.

               704 Il n'y a pas de plaisir sans peine.
                    No pleasure without pain.

               705 Plaisir non partagé n'est plaisir qu'à demi.
                    A joy that's shared is a joy made double.
                    Happiness is not perfect until it is shared.

---

*   Unlike the English Proverb, the French exalts constancy,
          construing moss as something positive or desirable, i.e. wealth,
          that cannot be ammassed through rambling.

| Plant | 706 | Il est plus facile de plier un jeune plant que de redresser un arbre. *Best to bend while it is green. As the twig is bent, so the tree is inclined.* |

Plant

706 Il est plus facile de plier un jeune plant que de redresser un arbre.
Best to bend while it is green. As the twig is bent, so the tree is inclined.

Plante

707 De noble plante, noble fruit.
The fruit of a good tree is also good.

Plier

708 Il vaut mieux plier que rompre.
Better bend than break.

Pluie

709 Après la pluie, le beau temps.
After rain comes sunshine.
After clouds, clear weather.

710 Ce sont les petites pluies qui gâtent les grands chemins.
Many sands will sink a ship.
†*Small rain lays great dust.*

711 Petite pluie abat grand vent.
A little rain stills a great wind.
Small rain allays great winds.

Plume

712 La belle plume fait le bel oiseau
Fair feathers make fair fowl.
Fine feathers make fine birds.

Poêle

713 Qui tient la poêle par la queue, il la tourne par où il lui plaît.
A rich man has the world by the tail.

Point

714 Un point fait à temps en épargne cent.
A stitch in time saves nine.

Poire

715 Il faut garder une poire pour la soif.
Save (lay up) for a rainy day.

716 Quand la poire est mûre, il faut qu'elle tombe.
The time to pick berries is when they're ripe.

Poisson   **717** Au poisson à nager ne montre.
Don't teach your grandmother to suck eggs.

718 De petite rivière de grand poisson n'espère.
Big fish are caught in a big river.
Little fish swim in shallow water.

719 En fleuve où manque le poisson, jeter filet est sans raison.
It is in vain to cast your net where there is no fish.

720 En grand torrent grand poisson se prend.
Great fish are caught in great waters.
Big fish are caught in a big river.

721 Les gros poissons mangent les petits.
The big fish eat the little ones.

722 L'hôtel et le poisson en trois jours sont poison.
Fish and guest (visitors) smell (stink) in three days.

723 Pas de poisson sans arête.
No land without stones, no meat without bones.

Pomme   **724** La pomme ne tombe pas loin du tronc.
The apple never falls far from the tree.

Pont   **725** Il faut faire un pont d'or à l'ennemi qui fuit.
For a flying enemy make a golden bridge.

Porte   **726** Il faut qu'une porte soit ouverte ou fermée.
A door must either be shut or open.

727 Que chacun balaie devant sa porte et les rues se-
ront nettes.
If each would sweep before his own door, we
should have a clean city (street).

Pot 728 A chaque pot son couvercle.
Every pot has its cover (lid).

729 C'est dans les vieux pots qu'on trouve les bonnes
soupes.
The best wine comes out of an old vessel.

730 Pot fêlé dure longtemps.
The cracked pot lasts the longest.

731 Qui vend le pot dit le mot.
Who will sell the cow must say the word.

Potier 732 Chaque potier vante son pot.
Every potter praises his own pot.

733 Le potier au potier porte envie.
One potter envies another.

Poule 734 Qui naît poule aime à gratter.
He that comes of a hen must scrape.

Pourceau 735 Nul ne peut donner des tripes sinon celui qui tue
son pourceau.
He who does not kill hogs, will not get black
puddings.

Pouvoir 736 Qui peut le plus, peut le moins.
The greater embraces (includes) the less.

Précaution 737 Deux précautions valent mieux qu'une.
A word before is worth two behind.

Premier	738	Le premier venu engrène.
		First come, first served.

Prendre	739	Qui prend, s'oblige (se vend).
		Benefits bind.
		Who receives a gift, sells his liberty.

Présent	740	A petit présent, petit merci.
		A small gift usually gets small thanks.
	741	Les petits présents entretiennent l'amitié.
		Friendship is a plant that must often be watered.

Prêtre	742	Chaque prêtre loue ses reliques.
		Each priest praises his own relics.
	743	Tel prêtre, tel peuple.
		Like priest, like people.

Prévenir	744	Il veut mieux prévenir que guérir.
		Prevention is better than cure.

Prière	745	Courtes prières pénètrent les cieux.
		A short prayer penetrates heaven.

Procureur	746	Celui qui agit par procureur est souvent trompé en personne.
		If you want a thing done, go; if not, send.

Profit	747	Chacun cherche son propre profit.
		Everyone fastens where there is gain.
	748	Petit profit emplit la bourse.
		Little and often fills the purse.

Proie	749	Il ne faut pas laisser la proie pour l'ombre. He who grabs at the shadow may lose the substance.
Promesse	750	Entre promesse et l'effet 'y a grand trait. *Between promising and performing, a man may marry his daughter.*
Promettre	751	Promettre et tenir son deux. It is one thing to promise, another to perform.
Prophète	752	Nul n'est prophète en son pays. No man is a prophet in his own country.
Propos	753	Les longs propos font les courts jours. *Sweet discourse makes short days and nights.* *Cheerful company shortens the miles.*
Propre	754	Qui est propre à tout n'est propre à rien. *Jack of all trades, master of none.*
Prospérité	755	Le vent de prospérité change bien souvent de côté. *Fortune is fickle.*
Prouver	756	Qui prouve trop ne prouve rien. He that proves too much proves nothing.
Prudence	757	Prudence est mère de sûreté. Caution is the parent of safety.
Puits	758	Ne crachez pas dans le puits, vous pouvez en boire l'eau. Do not spit into the well you may have to drink out of.

Punition   759 La punition boîte mais elle arrive.
                       Punishment is lame, but it comes.
                       Punishment comes slowly, but it comes.

R

Racine   760 Telle racine, telle feuille.
                        Like tree, like fruit.

Raillerie   761 Il n'est pire raillerie que la véritable.
                        There is no worse jest than a true one.

                  762 La raillerie ne doit point passer le jeu.
                        Don't carry a joke too far.

Raison   763 En trop parler n'a pas raison.
                        Talk much and err much.

                  764 La raison du plus fort est toujours la meilleure.
                        Might overcomes right.

                  765 Raison fait maison.
                        Reason rules all things.

Rat   766 Rat (la souris) qui n'a qu'un trou est vite pris(e).
                        The mouse that has but one hole is soon caught.

                  767 Tel rat, tel chat.
                        A bad cat deserves a bad rat.

Receleur   768 Le receleur ne vaut pas mieux que le voleur.
                        The receiver is as bad as the thief.

Règle

769 Il n'y a pas de règle sans exception.
(Toute règle a ses exceptions.)
There's no rule without an exception.

770 Mieux vaut règle que rente.
Sparing is the first gaining.

Remède

771 Le meilleur remède des injures c'est de les
mépriser.
The best remedy for an injury is to forget it.

772 Le remède est souvent pire que le mal.
The remedy (cure) may be worse than the disease.

773 On trouve remède à tout, excepté la mort.
There is a remedy for all things but death.

Renard

774 A la fin, le renard sera moine.
At length the fox turns monk.

775 Avec le renard, on renarde.
One must howl with the wolves.

776 Le renard cache sa queue.
The tail does often catch the fox.

777 Le renard est pris, lâchez vos poules.
When the fox dies, fowls do not mourn.

778 Le renard prêche aux poules.
When the fox preaches, beware of your geese.

779 Renard qui dort la matinée n'a pas la gueule em-
plumée.
The sleepy fox has seldom feathered breakfasts.

780 Un bon renard ne mange pas les poules de son
voisin.
The fox preys farthest from his home (den).

781 Un renard n'est pas pris deux fois à un piège.
A fox is not caught twice in the same place.

Renom	782	Bon renom vaut même un héritage.
		A good reputation is better than money.
Renommée	783	Bonne renommée vaut mieux que ceinture dorée.
		A good name is better than gold.
Repentir	784	Qui se repent est presque innocent.
		Repentance is good, but innocence is better.
Ressembler	785	Qui se ressemble, s'assemble.
		(Ceux qui se ressemblent s'assemblent.)
		Birds of a feather flock together.
Riche	786	Du riche, prospère et opulent, chacun est cousin et parent.
		Everyone is akin to the rich man.
	787	N'est pas riche celui qui a du bien, mais celui qui sait se contenter.
		He is not rich that possesses much, but he that is content with what he has.
	788	On est assez riche quand on a le nécessaire.
		He is rich enough that wants nothing. He is rich who doesn't desire more.
	789	Tout le monde ne peut pas être riche.
		Everyone can't be first.
Richesse	790	Il n'est richesse que de science et santé.
		Good health and good sense are two of life's greatest blessings.
Rien	791	Il n'y a que celui qui ne fait rien qui ne se trompe pas.
		He who never made a mistake never made nothing. Who does nothing can do nothing wrong.

792 On ne fait rien de rien.
     Nothing comes of (from) nothing.

793 On ne fait rien pour rien.
     Nothing happens for nothing.

794 Qui ne risque rien n'a rien.
     Nothing ventured, nothing gained.

795 Qui rien ne sait, de rien ne doute.
     He that knows nothing, doubts nothing.

796 Rien ne se perd, rien ne se crée.
     Matter can neither be created nor destroyed.

Rire

797 Au rire connaît-on le fol et le niais.
     A loud laugh bespeaks the vacant (hollow) mind.
     Laughter is the hiccup of a fool.

798 Celui qui rit toujours trompe souvent.
     There are daggers behind men's smiles.
     A smiling boy seldom proves a good servant.

799 Rira bien qui rira le dernier.
     He laughs best who laughs last.

800 Trop rire fait pleurer.
     After laughter (through), (come) tears.

Rivière

801 La rivière ne grossit pas sans être trouble.
     Muck and money go together.

Rinière

802 Les rivières retournent à la mer
     All rivers run to the sea.

Robe

803 Tailler la robe selon le corps.
     Cut your coat according to your cloth.

| Roi | 804 | Aujourd'hui roi, demain rien. |
| | | *Today a man, tomorrow none.* |

| | 805 | Il ne faut pas être plus royaliste que le roi. |
| | | More royalist than the king. |

| | 806 | Il ne parle pas au roi qui veut. |
| | | *Only the eagle can gaze at the sun.* |

| | 807 | Les rois ont les mains longues. |
| | | Kings have long arms. |

| | 808 | Nouveaux rois (maîtres), nouvelles lois. |
| | | New lords, new laws. |

| Rome | 809 | En demandant, on va à Rome. |
| | | *He who uses his tongue shall reach his destination.* |

| | 810 | Il faut vivre à Rome selon les coutumes romaines. |
| | | When in Rome, do as the Romans. |

| | 811 | Qui veut vivre à Rome, ne doit pas se quereller avec le pape. |
| | | It is hard to live in Rome and strive against the Pope. |

| | 812 | Rome (Paris) ne fut pas faite en un jour. |
| | | *Rome (Paris) was not built in one day.* |

| Rose | 813 | Il n'y a point de (nulle) rose sans épines. |
| | | No rose without a thorn. |

| Rossignol | 814 | Quand le rossignol a vu ses petits, il ne chante plus. |
| | | *Children are certain cares, but uncertain comforts.* |

| Roue | 815 | La maîtresse roue fait tourner le moulin. |
| | | *Great engines turn on small pivots.* |

816 La plus méchante roue crie le plus.
The worst wheel of the cart makes the most
noise.

Ruisseau 817 Les petits ruisseaux font les grandes rivières.
Little streams make big rivers.

Ruse 818 Mieux vaut ruse (subtilité) que force.
Cunning surpasses strength.

S

Sac

819 Autant pèche celui qui tient le sac que celui qui l'emplit (met dedans).
He who holds the ladder is as bad as the thief.

820 D'un sac à charbon, il ne saurait sortir blanche farine.
He who touches pitch will get black. Only the witless expect a blacksmith to wear a white silk apron.

821 Il faut lier le sac avant qu'il soit plein.
Bind the sack before it be full.

822 Il ne sort du sac que ce qu'il a.
There comes nothing out of the sack but what was in it.

823 On frappe sur le sac pour que l'âne le sente.
He that cannot beat the ass beats the saddle.

Sage

824 Il n'est si sage qui ne foloie.
None so wise but the fool overtakes him.

825 Il n'y a si sage qui parfois ne rage.
A wise man may sometimes play the fool. *No man is always wise.*

826 Le sage se conforme à la vie de ses compagnons.
A wise man esteems every place to be his own country.

827 Les plus sages faillent souvent en bon chemin.
The wisest man may fall.

828 On est toujours sage après coup.
It is easy to be wise after the event.

829 Sage est qui fait de son tort droit.
Show a good man his error, he turns it to a virtue.

Sagesse

830 Mieux vaut sagesse que richesse.
Better wit than wealth.

831 Sagesse et grand avoir sont rarement en un manoir.
Riches and virtue seldom settle on one man. The love of money and the love of learning rarely meet.

832 Sagesse vaut mieux que force.
Wisdom is better than strength.

833 Toute la sagesse n'est pas enfermée dans une tête.
Two minds are better than one.

Saint

834 A chaque saint sa chandelle.
Honour to whom honour is due.

835 A petit saint, petite offrande.
Like saint, like offering.

Sang

836 Bon sang ne peut mentir.
Blood is thicker than water.

Santé

837 Qui n'a santé, il n'a rien; qui a santé, il a tout.
If you lack health, you lack everything.

838 Santé passe richesse.
Health is better than wealth.

Sauce

839 Il n'est sauce que d'appétit.
     Appetite is the best sauce.

Savoir

840 De savoir vient avoir.
     Trade is the mother of money.

841 Savoir, c'est pouvoir.
     Knowledge is power.

Science

842 Grande science est folie si bon sens ne la guide.
     Knowledge is folly, except where grace guides it.

843 La science de l'ignorant, c'est de reprendre les
     choses bien dites.
     Wise men make proverbs, fools repeat them.

Secret

844 Secret de deux, secret de Dieu; secret de trois,
     secret de tous.
     *A secret is too little for one, enough for two, too
     much for three.*

Seigneur

845 A tout seigneur tout honneur.
     Honour to whom honour is due.
     Give credit to whom credit is due.

846 En l'absence du seigneur se connaît le serviteur.
     A servant is known by his master's absence.

847 Qui avec son seigneur mange poires, il ne choisit
     pas les meilleures.
     *Share not pears with your master either in jest or
     earnest.*

848 Tant vaut le seigneur (l'homme), tant vaut la
     terre.
     The master's footsteps fatten the soil.

849 Un grand seigneur, un grand clocher, une grande rivière sont trois mauvais voisins.
A great man and a great river are often ill neighbours.

Sel

850 Sel et conseil ne se donnent qu'à celui qui les demande.
Give neither salt nor advice till you are asked for it.

Semer

851 Il faut semer pour recueillir (qui veut moissoner).
No sowing, no reaping.

852 Le semer et la moisson ont leur temps et leur saison.
There is a time to reap and a time to sow.

853 Qui partout sème ne récolte nulle part.
Sow thin and mow thin.

854 Qui sème tôt emplit son grenier.
Early sow, early mow.

Service

855 Beau service fait amis, vrai dire ennemis.
Truth finds foes where it makes none.

856 Service d'autrui n'est pas héritage.
A trade is better than service.

Servir

857 On n'est jamais si bien servi que par soi-même.
If you would be well served, serve yourself.

Seul

858 Il vaut mieux être seul qu'en mauvaise compagnie (que mal accompagné).
Better alone than in bad company.

859 Quand on est seul on devient nécessaire.
He that has but one eye must be afraid to lose it.

| Sien | 860 | A chacun le sien ce n'est pas trop. |
| | | *Every man likes his own thing best.* |

| | 861 | On n'est jamais trahi que par les siens. |
| | | *There is falsehood in fellowship.* |

| Sifflet | 862 | Si vous n'avez pas d'autre sifflet, votre chien est perdu. |
| | | *Don't put all your eggs in one basket.* |

| Singe | 863 | Un singe vêtu de pourpre est toujours un singe. |
| | | *An ape's an ape, a varlet's a varlet, though they be clad in silk or scarlet.* |

| Soif | 864 | Plus on boit, plus on a soif. |
| | | The more you drink, the more you want. |

| Soleil | 865 | Là où entre le soleil, le médecin n'entre pas. |
| | | Where the sun enters, the doctor does not. |

| | 866 | Le soleil luit pour tout le monde. |
| | | The sun shines on all the world. |

| Songe | 867 | Songes sont mensonges. |
| | | Dreams are lies. |

| Sot | 868 | A sot auteur, sot admirateur. |
| | | *A fool always finds a bigger fool to praise him. One fool praises another.* |

| | 869 | Les sots sont heureux. |
| | | Ignorance is bliss. *Fools are never uneasy.* |

| Souhait | 870 | Si souhaits étaient des chevaux, les mendiants seraient garçons d'écurie. |
| | | If wishes were horses, beggars might ride. |

Soulier	871	Qui attend les souliers d'un mort risque d'aller pieds nus. *He that waits for a dead man's shoes may go a long time barefoot.*
Soumission	872	La soumission désarme la colère. *A soft answer turns away wrath.*
Soupe	873	La soupe fait le soldat. *An army marches on its stomach.*
	874	On fait de bonne soupe dans un vieux pot. *Good broth may be made in an old pot.*
	875	Qui se lève tard trouve la soupe froide. *He that comes last to the pot is soonest wroth. Who comes late, lodges ill.*
Sourd	876	Il n'est pire sourd que celui qui ne veut entendre. *None so deaf as they that will not hear.*
Subtilité	877	Mieux vaut subtilité que force. *Reason succeeds where force fails.* *Discretion is the better part of valour.*
Surplus	878	Le surplus rompt le couvercle. *The last straw will break the camel's back.*

T

Table 879 La table est l'entremetteuse de l'amitié.
When meat is in, anger is out.
Spread the table and contention will cease.

Taillis 880 Au fond du taillis sont les mûres.
Fairest gems lie deepest.
The best fishing is in the deepest waters.

Tambour 881 A bon tambour, bonne baguette.
If you give a jest, you must take a jest.
Like fault, like punishment.

Tard 882 Il n'est jamais trop tard pour bien faire.
Never too late to do well.

883 Il vaut mieux tard que jamais.
Better late than never.

Temps 884 Après bon temps, on se repent.
Rejoice today and repent tomorrow.
Short pleasure often brings long repentance.

885 Avec du temps et de la patience, on vient à bout de tout.
Patience, time and money accomodate all things.

886 Changement de temps, entretien de sot.
Change of weather is the discourse of fools.

887 Il faut prendre le temps comme il vient.
Take time when it comes.
Take time when time comes, lest time steal away.

888 Il viendra un temps où les vaches (chiens) auront besoin de leur queue.
Cows don't know the good of their tail till fly time.
The cow knows not the value of her tail till she has lost it.

889 Il y a temps pour tout.
There is a time for everything.

890 Il y a un temps de parler et un temps de se taire.
There is a time to speak and a time to be silent.

891 Le temps dévore tout.
Time devours all things.

892 Le temps est un grand maître.
Time is a great teacher. Time is a hard taskmaster.

893 Qui a temps a vie.
He that has time has life.

Tenir

894 Il vaut mieux tenir que courir.
Better to have than to wish.

895 Quand on est bien, il faut s'y tenir.
We do not always gain by changing.
He is wise that knows when he is well enough.

896 Un tiens vaut mieux que deux tu l'auras.
Better is one "Accipe" than twice to say "Dabo tibi."

Tentation	897	Le plus sûr moyen de vaincre la tentation c'est d'y succomber.

The best way to resist temptation is to give in to it.

Terme	898	Le terme vaut l'argent.

Time is capital, invest it wisely.

Terre	899	Bonnes terres, mauvais chemins.

Good land, (where there is) evil (foul) way.

900 Nulle terre sans guerre.
He that has lands has war (quarrels).

901 Six pieds de terre suffisent au plus grand homme.
Six feet of earth make all men equal.

Tête	902	Autant de têtes, autant d'avis.

So many heads, so many wits.

903 En petite tête gît grand sens.
Small head, big ideas.

904 Grosse tête, peu de sens.
Big head, little sense.

905 Quand on n'a pas de bonne tête, il faut avoir bonnes jambes.
What you haven't got in your head, you have in your feet.

906 Qui a tête de cire ne doit pas s'approcher du feu.
If your head is wax, do not walk in the sun.

Titre	907	Le titre ne fait pas le maître.

Masters are made, not born.

Ton	908	C'est le ton qui fait la chanson (musique).

The sound makes the song.

| Tonneau | 909 | Ce sont les tonneaux vides qui font le plus de bruit. |
| | | *Empty barrels make the most noise.* |

Tonner	910	Quand il tonne, il faut écouter tonner.
		What can't be cured must be endured.
		We must bear and forebear.
	911	Toutes les fois qu'il tonne, le tonnere ne tombe pas.
		When the thunder is very loud, there's very little rain.

| Travail | 912 | Qui hait le travail, hait la vertu. |
| | | *Idleness is the root of all evil.* |

| Tristesse | 913 | De tristesse et ennui nul fruit. |
| | | *Sorrow is good for nothing but sin.* |

| Trompeur | 914 | Aujourd'hui trompeur, demain trompé. |
| | | *Cheats never prosper. The biter is sometimes bit.* |

Trop	915	Mieux vaut trop que trop peu.
		Better too much than too little.
	916	Souvent tombe qui trop galope.
		They stumble that run fast.

Trou	917	A petit trou, petite cheville.
		The hole and the patch should be commensurate.
	918	Autant de trous, autant de chevilles.
		Success comes in rising every time you fall.
	919	Qui ne rapièce un petit trou en rapiècera des grands.
		He that corrects not small faults, will not control great ones.

Tuer   920 Tel tue qui ne pense que frapper.
                         He often kills that thinks but to hurt.

U

Union	921	L'union fait la force. In union there is strength.
Usage	922	L'usage fait loi. Custom has the force of law.
	923	Usage rend maître. Use makes mastery.

V

Vache   924 Les vaches qui remuent tant la queue, ce ne sont
                        pas celles qui ont le plus de lait.
                        *It isn't the cow that lows the most that will give the
                        most milk.*

                   925 Qui mange la vache du roi, à cent ans de là en
                        paie les os.
                        *He that eats the king's goose shall be choked with
                        the feathers.*

                   926 Vache de loin a assez de lait.
                        Faraway cows have long horns.

Vairon   927 Il faut perdre un vairon pour pêcher un saumon.
                        Venture a small fish to catch a great one.
                        *Throw out a sprat to catch a herring. A hook's well
                        lost to catch a salmon.*

Valet   928 Autant de valets, autant d'ennemis.
                        So many servants, so many enemies.

Vanité   929 La vanité est la mère du mensonge.
                        The vaunter and the liar are near akin.
                        The greater the flattery, the bigger the liar.

930 La vanité n'a pas de plus grand ennemi que la
vanité.
The proud hate pride in others.
Pride with pride will not abide.

Vanteur   931 Grand vanteur, petit faiseur.
Great braggers, little doers.
Great boast, small roast.

Vase   932 Quand le vase est trop plein, il faut qu'il déborde.
Too much in the vessel bursts its lid.

Veau   933 Autant meurt veau que vache.
Death devours lambs as well as sheep.

Vendredi   934 Tel qui rit vendredi dimanche pleurera.
Laugh before breakfast, cry before sunset.

Vengeance   935 La vengeance est le plaisir des dieux.
Revenge is a morsel for God.

936 La vengeance est un plat qui se mange froid.
Revenge is a dish that can be eaten cold.

Vent   937 Il faut laisser courir le vent par-dessus les tuiles.
What can't be cured must be endured.

938 Il faut que le vent soit bien mauvais pour n'être
bon à personne.
It is an ill wind that blows nobody good.

939 Qui pisse contre le vent mouille sa chemise.
Who spits against the wind spits in his own face.

940 Qui sème le vent récolte la tempête.
Sow the wind and reap the whirlwind.

941 Selon (suivant) le vent, la voile.
As the wind blows, (you must) set your sail(s).

942 Vent au visage rend l'homme sage.
     The wind in one's face makes one wise.

Ventre   943 A ventre soûl, cerises amères.
                      When the cat's full, the milk tastes sour.
                      Too much honey cloys the stomach.

                 944 Tout fait ventre.
                      All's good in a famine.

                 945 Ventre affamé n'a point d'oreilles.
                      A hungry stomach (belly) has no ears.

                 946 Ventre affamé prend tout en gré.
                      Hunger never saw bad food (bread).

                 947 Ventre plein donne de l'assurance.
                      A full belly makes a brave heart.

Ver   948 Il faut toujours tendre un ver pour avoir une
                      truite.
                      A hook's well lost to catch a salmon.

                 949 Il y a un ver dans chaque pomme.
                      The rose has its thorn, the peach its worm.

Vérité   950 Il n'y a que la vérité qui blesse (offense).
                      The truth hurts.
                      It is truth that makes a man angry.

                 951 La vérité en deçà, erreur au-delà.
                      An hour perhaps divides the false and truth.

                 952 La vérité est dans le vin.
                      In wine there is truth.

                 953 La vérité se cache au fond d'un puits.
                      Truth lies at the bottom of a well.

                 954 La vérité sort de la bouche des enfants.
                      If you want the truth, ask a child.

955 Qui dit toute la vérité finit pendu au gibet.
Confess and be hanged.

956 Toute(s) vérité(s) n'est (ne sont) pas bonne(s) à dire.
All truths must not be told at all times.

957 Vérité engendre haine.
Truth breeds hatred.

Verre

958 Qui casse les verres les paie.
He pays for the glasses who breaks them.

Vertu

959 La vertu trouve toujours sa récompense.
Goodness is the only investment that never fails.
A good deed is never lost. Honour is the reward of virtue.

960 Vertu excelle force.
It is not strength but art that obtains the prize.

961 Vertu gît au milieu.
Virtue is found in the middle (mean).

Viande

962 Il n'y a point de viande sans os.
Bone brings meat to town.

963 Nouvelle viande donne goût.
New meat, new appetite.
New dishes beget new appetites.

964 Viande d'ami est bientôt prête.
He is free of fruit that wants an orchard.

965 Vieille viande fait bonne soupe.
Good broth may be made in an old pot.

Vie

966 De mauvaise vie, mauvaise fin.
An ill life, an ill end.

967 Nous n'avons que notre vie en ce monde.
You don't have to do anything but live till you die.

968 Tant qu'il y a de la vie, il y a de l'espoir.
While there's life, there's hope.

969 Telle vie, telle mort.
Such a life, such a death.

970 Vie de cochon, courte et bonne.
He that lives carnally won't live eternally.

Vieillir

971 Il faut vieillir ou mourir jeune.
Old be or young die.
*The way never to grow old and grey headed is to
die young. If you would not live to be old, you must
be hanged when you are young.*

Vieux

972 Il faut devenir vieux de bonne heure, si on veut
l'être longtemps.
Young old and old long.
An old young man will be a young old man.

973 Plus on est vieux, plus on est bête.
 The older, the worse. *Age makes a man white but
not better.*

Vilain

974 Vilain enrichi ne connaît parent ni ami.
As the carl riches, he wretches.

Ville

975 Toute ville qui parlemente est à moitié rendue.
A city that parleys is half gotten.

Vin

976 A bon vin point d'enseigne.
Good wine needs no bush.

977 Bon vin, mauvaise tête.
*Sweet's the wine, but sour's the payment.
Drinking and thinking don't mix.*

978 Chaque vin a sa lie.
No silver without its dross.
No garden without its weeds.

979 Le bon vin réjouit le coeur de l'homme.
Good wine engenders good blood.

980 Le vin entre et la raison sort.
When wine is in, wit is out.

981 Le vin est le lait des vieillards.
Wine is old men's milk.

982 Le vin est tiré, il faut le boire.
The wine is drawn, it must be drunk.

983 Le vin est un bon valet mais un fichu maître.
Whiskey - a good servant but a bad master.

984 Qui vin ne boit après salade, est en danger d'être malade.
He that drinks not wine after salad, is in danger of being sick.

985 Vin sur lait bienfait, lait sur vin venin.
Milk says to wine, "Welcome friend."

986 Vin versé n'est pas avalé.
Spilt wine is worse than water.

Violent

987 Tout ce qui est violent n'est pas durable.
Nothing that is violent is permanent.

Vivre

988 On ne sait qui vit ni qui meurt.
Death keeps no calendar.
No man has a lease on his life.

989 Pour vivre heureux, vivons cachés.
He lives well that lives closely (has lurked).

990 Qui vit en paix dort en repos.
A good conscience is a soft pillow.

Voir	**991**	Un vu vaut mieux que cent entendus. *One eyewitness is better than ten hearsays.*
Voisin	**992**	Qui a bon voisin a bon matin. *A good neighbour, a good morrow.*
Vol	**993**	Il faut mesurer son vol à ses ailes. *Make not your sail too large for your ship.*
Voleur	**994**	Les grands voleurs pendent les petits. *The big thieves hang the little ones.*
	995	On pend les petits voleurs mais on épargne les grands. *We hang little thieves and take off our hats to great ones.*
Volonté	**996**	A bonne volonté ne faut la faculté. *Nothing is impossible to a willing heart. He who wills the end, wills the means.*
	997	La bonne volonté est réputée pour le fait. *Acts indicate intentions.*
Vouloir	**998**	A qui veut assez rien ne faut. *He has enough who is contented with little.*
	999	Vouloir, c'est pouvoir. *Where there's a will there's a way.*
Vrai	**1000**	Le vrai peut quelquefois n'être pas vraisemblable. *Fact (truth) is stranger than fiction.*

Bibliography

Asceaux, Marcel. *Ah! Ces proverbes*. Rodez.

Belcour, G. *A Selection of the Most Used French Proverbs with English Equivalents*. London: 1882.

Benas, B.L. "On the Proverbs of European Nations." *Proceedings of the Literary and Philosophical Society of Liverpool*. no.32 (1877-78), 291-332.

Buridant, Claude (ed.). "Rhétorique du proverbe." *Revue des sciences humaines*, 41, no.163 (1976), 309-436.

Champion, Selwyn Gurney. *Racial Proverbs: A Selection of the World's Proverbs, Arranged Linguistically with Authoritative Introductions to the Proverbs of 27 Countries and Races*. London: Routledge & Kegan, 1963.

Dournon, Jean-Yves. *Le dictionnaire des proverbes et dictons de France*. Hachette, 1986.

Friesland, Carl. "Französische Sprichwörter-Bibliographie." *Zeitschrift für französische Sprache und Literatur*, 28 (1905), 260-287.

Glaap, Albert-Reiner and Weller, Franz-Rudolf. "Auswahlbibliographie zur Idiomatik im Fremdsprachenunterricht (Englisch/Französisch)." *Die Neueren Sprachen*, 78 (1979), 586-595.

Greimas, Algirdas-Julien. "Idiotismes, proverbes, dictons." *Cahiers de Lexicologie*, 2 (1960), 41-61.

Guiraud, Pierre. *Les locutions françaises*. Paris: Presses Universitaires de France, 1961. 4th edition, 1973.

Lamesangère. *Dictionnaire des proverbes français*. 1821.

Maloux, Maurice. *Dictionnaire des proverbes, sentences et maximes*. Paris: Larousse, 1993.

McKay, D. *National Proverbs: France*. Philadelphia: 1920.

Meurier. *Recueil des sentences notables et dictons communs*. 1568, reed.1617.

Mieder W., Kingsbury S.A., Harder K.B. *A Dictionary of American Proverbs*. Oxford: OUP, 1992.

O'Kane, Eleanor S. "The Proverb: Rabelais and Cervantes." *Comparative Literature*, 2 (1950), 360-369.

Panckoucke. *Dictionnaire des proverbes français*. 1749.

Payen-Payne, J.B. *French Idioms and Proverbs*. Oxford:1924.

Pineaux, Jacques. *Proverbes et dictons français*. Paris: Presses Universitaires de France, 1956 (6th ed. 1973).

Quitard, Pierre-Marie. *Dictionnaire étymologique, historique, et anecdotique des proverbes et des locutions proverbiales de la langue française*. Paris, 1842.

Rivard, Adjutor. "A propos de proverbes." *Le Canada français*, 4 (1920), 400-407.

Roy, Claude. "La sagesse des nations." In id. *L'Homme en question*. Paris: Gallimard, 1960. 39-49.

Singer, Samuel. *Sprichwörter des Mittelalters*. 3 vols. Bern: Herbert Lang, 1944-47.

Suringar, Willem Hendrik Dominikus. *Erasmus over nederlandsche spreekwoorden en spreekwoorderlijke uitdrukkingen van zijnen tijd, uit's mans «Adagia» opgezameld en uit andere, meest nieure geschriften opgehelderd*. Utrecht: Kemink, 1873.

Tallgren-Tuulio, O.J. "Locutions figurées calquées et non calqués. Essai de classification pour une série de langues littéraires." *Mémoires de la société néo-philologique de Helsingfors*, 9 (1932), 279-324.

Taylor, Archer. *The Proverb*. Cambridge, Mass.: Harvard University Press, 1931.

Tordoir, M. "Etude critique de quelques proverbes de Littré." *Cahiers de littéraure de linguistique appliquée*, 2 (1970), 203-218 and 5-6 (1972), 73-92.

Whiting, Bartlett Jere. "Proverbs in Certain Middle English Romances in Relation to their French Sources." *Harvard Studies and Notes in Philology and Literature*. 15 (1933), 75-126.

Wilson, F.P. *The Oxford Dictionary of English Proverbs* 3rd. ed. Oxford: OUP, 1970.

English Key Word Index

NB Index entries are arranged by *key word*, by which is meant the sequentially first noun most closely associated with the meaning of the proverb and/or having greater linguistic range or frequency. For proverbs without nouns, key words are verbs, adjectives or adverbs used on the basis of the same criteria. All numbers refer to the numbers of the French proverb entries, not pages.

FRENCH LANGUAGE TITLES
FROM HIPPOCRENE . . .

MASTERING FRENCH
by E.J. Neather
A useful tool for language learning, this method combines a full-size text with two audio cassettes allowing learners to hear proper pronunciation by native speakers as they study the book.
Book:
288 pgs, 5 1/2 x 81 /2
0-87052-055-5
$11.95pb (511)
2 Cassettes:
0-87052-060-1
$12.95 (512)

MASTERING ADVANCED FRENCH
by E.J. Neather
An advanced course of French utilizing the method of *Mastering French.*
Book:
278 pages, 5 1 2/ x 8 1/2
0-7818-0312-8
$14.95pb (0041)
2 Cassettes:
0-7818-0313-6
$12.95 (0054)

FRENCH HANDY DICTIONARY

For the traveler of independent spirit and curious mind, this practical dictionary will help you to communicate, not just get by. Common phrases are conveniently listed through key words. Pronunciation follows each entry and a reference section reviews all major grammar points.
120 pages, 5 x 7 3/4
0-7818-0010-2
$8.95pb (0155)

FRENCH-ENGLISH/ ENGLISH-FRENCH PRACTICAL DICTIONARY
with Larger Print
by Rosalind Williams
386 pages, 5 1/2 x 8 1 /4
35,000 entries
0-7818-0178-8
$9.95pb (0199)

TREASURY OF FRENCH LOVE POEMS, QUOTATIONS AND PROVERBS
in FRENCH and ENGLISH
edited and translated by Richard Branyon

A bilingual gift collection of popular French love poems spanning eight centuries. Works from Baudelaire, Hugo, Rimbaud and others offer insight into the French perspective on romance.
128 pages, 5 x 7
0-7818-0307-1
$11.95hc (344)
Audiobook:
0-7818-0359-4
$12.95 (580)

500 FRENCH WORDS AND PHRASES FOR CHILDREN
written and edited by Carol Watson and Philippa Moyle
This book uses colorful cartons to teach children basic French
phrases and vocabulary.
32 pages, 8 x 10, full color illustrations
0-7818-0267-9
$8.95 (37)

FRENCH LITERATURE FROM HIPPOCRENE. . .

THE MARQUISE DE SADE
Rachilde (Marguerite Emery)
translated by Liz Heron
Mary Barbe, the orphaned daughter of a cavalry officer, is sent to
live with her elderly uncle, a scientist. In a family where only the
male sex is prized, she leads a life of seclusion until the approach
of her womanhood. Her beauty, learning, and a streak of
ruthlessness combine to give her the means to carve out a place in
the world and exact cruel dues as revenge.
336 pages, 5 1/2 x 8 1/2
1-873982-06-2
$16.95pb (0417)

ANGELS OF PERVERSITY
Remy de Gourmont
The short works in this volume are case studies in sexual attraction
and the bizarre behaviors which result.
192 pages, 5 x 8
0-946626-81-2
$11.95pb (0420)

LE CALVAIRE
Octave Mirbeau
This thinly veiled autobiographical novel paints a nightmarish
picture of late 19th century French society: from the emotional
sterility of family life and the stultifying boredom of bourgeois
provincialism to the horrors of the Franco-Prussian war.
256 pages, 5 1/2 x 8 1/2
0-944626-99-5
$16.95pb (0077)

MICROMEGAS AND OTHER STORIES
Voltaire
A delightful collection of 18th century science fiction in the form
of travelogues.
192 pages, 5 x 8
0-946626-55-3
$11.95pb (0424)

MONSIEUR DE PHOCAS
Jean Lorrain
Monsieur de Phocas ranks with *A Rebours* as the summation of the
French decadence movement. Modeled on *The Picture of Dorian
Gray*, it drips with evil.
320 pgaes, 5 1/2 x 8 1/4
1-873982-15-1
$14.95pb (0416)

SCUM OF THE EARTH
Arthur Koestler
"Koestler's personal history of France at War (WWII). It is, I
think, the finest book that has come out of that cauldron." — *New
York Herald Tribune*
288 pages, 5 1/2 x 8 1/2
0-90787-107-0
$14.95pb (506)

SERAPHITA AND OTHER STORIES
Honré de Balzac
Seraphita is an angelic and mysterious hermaphrodite, who
inspires love in all she meets. The battle for her affection leads
Wilf and Manna past earthly knowledge into the deeper mysteries
of life. Set in 18th century Norway, this bizarre novel reveals a
side of Balzac's genius unknown to most readers.
316 pages, 5 x 8
1-873982-41-0
$14.95pb (545)

TORTURE GARDEN
Octave Mirbeau
Clara, mistress to a Frenchman, scorns society which she feels tortures people in unseen ways, preferring the visible tortures she sees inflicted amid a Chinese flower garden she has discovered. Strewn with bodies, this flower garden flourishes with human compost.
296 pages, 5 x 8
1-873982-51-8
$16.95pb (0327)

UNDINE
La Motte-Fouque
Set in the Golden Age of Nordic chivalry, this Romantic classic, extolled by Goth and Heine, draws out the mystical and the erotic from traditional folklore.
224 pages, 5 x 8
0-94662-657-X
$11.95pb (0400)

FRENCH TRAVEL WITH HIPPOCRENE. . .

PARIS INSIDER'S GUIDE
Elaine Kline
"Just what English speaking visitors need to discover Paris. This
book shows remarkable knowledge of our capital as well as a deep
love for Paris." —*Jacques Chirac, President of France*
347 pages, 5 1/2 x 8 1/2
town plans, b/w photos, index
0-87052-876-9
$14.95pb   (0012)

THE FRENCH ANTILLES
Andy Gerald Gravette
The author conveys the exotic flavor of life in the tropics, as well
as the delicate and endearing romance of the culture for the
traveler, browser or fun-seeking vacationer.
246 pages, 5 1/4 x 9
index, maps, b/w pictures, illustrations
0-87052-105-5
$11.95pb (0085)

OVERLORD COASTLINE
The Major D-Day Locations
Stephen Chicken
This travel guide and military manual will show you with 87
photographs, and 37 maps and plans, what was happening where
on June 6, 1944.
104 pages, 5 1/2 x 8 1/2
0-7818-0274-1
 $14.95pb (0374)

(All prices subject to change.)

TO PURCHASE HIPPOCRENE BOOKS contact your local bookstore, or write to: HIPPOCRENE BOOKS, 171 Madison Ave, New York, NY 10016. Please enclose check or money order, adding $5.00 for shipping and handling (UPS) for the first book and ¢.50 for each additional book.

 **AUDIO·FORUM**
THE LANGUAGE SOURCE

Self-Taught Audio Language Courses

Hippocrene Books is pleased to recommend Audio-Forum self-taught language courses. They match up very closely with the languages offered in Hippocrene dictionaries and offer a flexible, economical and thorough program of language learning.

Audio-Forum audio-cassette/book courses, recorded by native speakers, offer the convenience of a private tutor, enabling the learner to progress at his or her own pace. They are also ideal for brushing up on language skills that may not have been used in years. In as little as 25 minutes a day — even while driving, exercising, or doing something else — it's possible to develop a spoken fluency.

French Self-Taught Language Courses

Basic French Part A 12 cassettes (15 hr.), 194-p. text, $185. Order #HF170.

Basic French Part B 18 cassettes (25 hr.), 290-p. text, $215. Order #HF181.

Basic French Advanced Level A Units 13-18. 18 cassettes (27 hr.), 567-p. text, $245. Order #HF260.

Basic French Advanced Level B Units 19-24. 18 cassettes (22 hr.), 567-p. text, $245. Order #HF290.

French for Business (Intermediate Course) 8 cassettes (45 min. each), 137-p. text, $185. Order #HFR225.

All Audio-Forum courses are fully guaranteed and may be returned within 30 days for a full refund if you're not completely satisfied.

You may order directly from Audio-Forum by calling toll-free 1-800-243-1234.

For a complete course description and catalog of 264 courses in 91 languages, contact Audio-Forum, Dept. SE5, 96 Broad St., Guilford, CT 06437. Toll-free phone 1-800-243-1234. Fax 203-453-9774.